Can We Ensure Safe Schools?

Also by Fern Aefsky
Collaborative Leadership: Building Capacity through Effective Partnerships

Can We Ensure Safe Schools?

A Collaborative Guide on Focused Strategies for School Safety

Edited by
Fern Aefsky

ROWMAN & LITTLEFIELD
Lanham • Boulder • New York • London

Published by Rowman & Littlefield
An imprint of The Rowman & Littlefield Publishing Group, Inc.
4501 Forbes Boulevard, Suite 200, Lanham, Maryland 20706
www.rowman.com

6 Tinworth Street, London SE11 5AL, United Kingdom

British Library Cataloguing in Publication Information Available

Library of Congress Cataloging-in-Publication Data Is Available
ISBN 978-1-4758-4518-1 (cloth: alk. paper)
ISBN 978-1-4758-4519-8 (pbk: alk. paper)
ISBN 978-1-4758-4520-4 (electronic)

♾™ The paper used in this publication meets the minimum requirements of American National Standard for Information Sciences—Permanence of Paper for Printed Library Materials, ANSI/NISO Z39.48-1992.

Printed in the United States of America

Contents

Foreword

This book provides research-based and pragmatic approaches that actually offer solutions with extensive lists of resources. It provides thoughtful discussion and provides practitioners solutions dealing with the reality of today's issues of school safety. Proactive steps, rather than only reactive ones, are extremely valuable for practitioners.

This book is a must-read tool for stakeholders in schools and school districts. The checklists and recommended plans of action are excellent tools to assess school and student needs and address all areas of school safety issues in an organized way.

As another school year begins, school personnel across the country are reviewing policies, practices, protocols, and procedures specifically in the area of school safety. The timing and information in this book are spot on.

In this day and age, so many are quick to decide that the only solution is to tackle the gun issue without offering any advice about prevention. The book gives background, research, and recommendations in a user-friendly way, for everyone from boards of education to community stakeholders.

This book provides the reader with a treasure trove of information to ensure all the bases are covered in keeping everyone at school safe. It is organized in a fashion where history, issues, and ameliorations are provided with surveys and sample policies.

Each member of a school community can use this book to inform, organize, and plan with their safety teams. The information in the book provides common language in an easy way for all to understand and implement.

As a director of Pupil Personnel Services, I am looking forward to working with the clinical staff members and the District School Safety Team citing parts of the book. Hopefully, in the future, we can do a book study as a group to plan for our future needs.

You offer solutions on many levels. Colleagues will greatly benefit from this book.

Dr. Edward Escobar
Director of Pupil Personnel Services
Bedford School District, NY

Preface

School safety is a concern of educators, parents, communities, and students. Each time there is a report of school shootings, members of the media, politicians, and all community stakeholders express their outrage, concern, and calls to action.

The mass shooting at Marjory Stoneman Douglas High School in Florida, on February 14, 2018, was another wake-up call to communities in the United States. Schools are supposed to be safe learning environments, and when parents send their children to school each day, they expect them to come home each night.

Unfortunately, when there is a school shooting, there is an outpouring of reactions and support. Sustainability, however, seems to fade within three months of each event.

The students of Marjory Stoneman Douglas High School took a stand and called for action, politically and bureaucratically. Once again, supportive reactions occurred. However, when another school shooting took place in Santa Fe, Texas, a few months later, May 18, news coverage was minimal after three days.

There have been 288 school shootings in the United States since 2009 where at least one person other than the shooter was shot (Grabow & Rose, 2018). This is unacceptable, and we, society at large, must take action to prevent further tragedies.

The issue of school safety is a critical one, and there are proactive measures that can be taken in school systems. This book identifies those proactive measures that should be considered by every school district, identifies ways to implement them, and describes specific measures for preventing school shootings. The book also identifies strategies and techniques that should be implemented when trauma does occur, and how building sustainable systems can assist all stakeholders.

The issue of school safety and school shootings will not go away, and implementation of techniques, strategies, and plans will assist school district personnel, families, and students in being prepared. Most importantly, dealing with mental health issues of students in a caring and proactive manner, so that situations are resolved before a student brings a gun to school, is a critical component of an effective plan.

State and federal tax dollars need to be prioritized for identifying and treating issues of mental health. Monies would be well spent on taking care of students' needs, which requires a cadre of assessment, intervention, and support for students.

We need all politicians and government officials to pay attention to the needs of students, personnel, and school districts when allocating funds for education. Students need to learn, teachers need to teach, and all need to be in a safe environment.

Readers of this book will have significant strategies and techniques that they can apply in their own schools, districts, and communities. Action must be taken, and now. Not one more student or stakeholder in a school setting should lose his or her life protecting students from a shooter on campus.

REFERENCE

Grabow, C., & Rose, L. (2018, May 21). The US has had 57 times as many school shootings as the other major industrialized nations combined. *CNN.* Retrieved October 25, 2018, from www.cnn.com/2018/05/21/us/school-shooting-us-versus-world-trnd/index.html.

Introduction

School shootings have occurred in elementary, middle, and high schools across the nation. Students do not feel safe in schools, and we—educators and other professionals—must inform politicians and bureaucrats that we are willing to work collaboratively in order to develop and implement plans for student welfare and safe learning environments.

This book was written as a guide to practitioners, with input and strategies from police authorities, mental health professionals, and educators. School safety is an issue for school communities across the country.

The strategies and plans discussed in this book are for students and school stakeholders, developed by a professional team of members from police authorities, social work, human services, and education backgrounds. The combined expertise provides a comprehensive look at what can be done proactively, actively, and reactively in response to incidents of school shootings.

Too often, a tragedy is the highlight of news media for a short period of time, and then everyone goes back to regular routines. There must be a constant and renewed ongoing discussion in every school community around school safety.

Mental health issues of students are often a catalyst for school shooters. There is a constant need for proactive intervention, and this book helps identify what resources are available and what school districts should do to assess and intervene with students in need of support. Too often, in the aftermath of a school shooting, the need for mental health support for the school shooter had been previously identified but not addressed sufficiently.

This cannot continue to occur, as our children and those adults working with our children in schools are at risk of harm. The strategies and guides provided in this book assist practitioners in schools, working with their local police authorities, in developing and implementing plans to address mental health issues, physical plant issues, and police issues, and most importantly, to keep our students, staff members, and schools safe.

Chapter 1

School Safety Needs

Fern Aefsky

During the first twenty-1 weeks of 2018, there were twenty-three school shootings where people were hurt or killed, an average of more than one shooting per week in the United States (Ahmed & Walker, 2018). These occurred in sixteen states, at the PK–12 and university levels. Since 1999, when the Columbine shooting occurred, there has been an average of ten shootings in schools per year; more than 187,000 students have been exposed to gun violence, and 130 people killed (students, family members, and educational staff) and over 254 people injured in school shootings (Cox & Rich, 2018).

School safety is a critical issue that needs immediate attention from every stakeholder in school communities across the country. On February 14, 2018, seventeen students and staff were killed and another seventeen wounded at Marjory Stoneman Douglas High School in Parkland, Florida. Students' response to this tragedy was powerful, and advocacy for gun control and action was vocal, visible, and constant. Media coverage was significant and ongoing.

However, on May 18, 2018, less than three months after the Parkland shooting, another shooting occurred at Santa Fe High School in Texas, where ten students and staff were killed and another ten wounded. On May 25, 2018, at a middle school in Indiana, three students and staff were shot. Media attention to these events was short-lived, indicating a possible level of acceptance that is of great concern to school and community members.

What follows is a list of four highly publicized school shootings since 1999:

- April 20, 1999, Columbine High School, Littleton, Colorado
  - Thirteen killed, more than twenty wounded
  - Two shooters, ages 18 and 17

- April 16, 2007, Virginia Tech University, Blacksburg, Virginia
  - Thirty-two people killed, more than twelve wounded
  - One shooter, age 23
- December 14, 2012, Sandy Hook Elementary School, Sandy Hook, Connecticut
  - Twenty-eight people killed, two injured
  - One shooter, age 20
- February 14, 2018, Marjory Stoneman Douglas High School, Parkland, Florida
  - Seventeen killed, seventeen wounded
  - One shooter, age 19

In these tragic events, the statistics above identify physical injuries. The emotional trauma these tragedies caused to many people who witnessed the events, people who were in the building, families of students involved and hurt, community members, as well as the families of the shooters, cannot be quantified by a number.

This book provides educators a comprehensive way of addressing pre-event, active, and post-event issues in planning appropriate mechanisms for dealing with potential and real trauma of school violence. Police authorities, mental health professionals, and educators are addressing the issue of school safety. The coordination, communication, and ongoing cycle of providing all stakeholders information is a challenge that must be overcome in order to provide safe learning environments.

School safety is a concern for students, parents, staff, faculty, administrators, and community stakeholders. Events in the media have a profound impact on issues that contribute to events in schools, making school personnel jobs more difficult, related to protecting the rights of all and managing a safe school environment. Laws, regulations, and policies must be clearly articulated and communicated so that school leaders have the necessary tools to ensure safe schools for all.

POLITICS OF SCHOOL SAFETY

Each tragic event involving students and school shootings, at both PK–12 and university campuses, resulted in a national discussion of political implications. The issues of Second Amendment rights, whether or not teachers should be armed, what our government should do regarding the passage of new laws, what type of guns should be available to all citizens (or not), what advocates should do to fight for the cause, and the need for quick action were discussed in every news media.

The Parkland students who survived the shooting in February 2018 took immediate action in response to their school and friends being the victim of an active shooting tragedy. They publicly called out the National Rifle Association's (NRA) political influence in the United States, and blamed their lobby for the nation's "lax gun laws" (Alter, 2018). They organized and pulled off a national protest just five weeks after the incident, and called for legislative action and solutions to what they called "an epidemic of mass shootings and the end to the influence of the NRA" (Grinberg & Muaddi, 2018). The students worked with the national media, holding news conferences and planning a march on Washington.

Their march had three main goals:

1. get legislators to pass a ban on assault weapons;
2. prohibit the sale of high-capacity magazines; and
3. require thorough background checks on all gun purchases, inclusive of gun shows and online purchases.

This movement began the #NeverAgain movement, and their primary focus was stated to be the initiators of continual pressure on gun control issues, as gun violence survivors.

Both federal and state government officials were approached, and called out for action specifically identified for supporters to pursue. Supporters aligned with these vocal students, and marches were held by thousands across the country and world in support of #NeverAgain.

Over eight hundred marches across the globe occurred in response, in various states in the United States and in England, Spain, Japan, Sweden, Denmark, and Italy. Students spoke eloquently and passionately about the need for change, and encouraged all students who were eligible to vote (eighteen years or older) to make sure their voices were heard in the next election cycle. Plans were made to honor the victims of the Columbine shooting on the nineteenth anniversary of that tragic event, April 20, by facilitating school walkouts, sit-ins, or rallies to ensure that voices were continually heard that action must be taken and taken now.

The president of the United States met with the students, parents, and teachers from Parkland within a week of the shooting. He expressed prayers and condolences to victims' families, and asked the group for ideas on how to stop gun violence in schools. "Stricter gun laws" was the prevalent response.

However, in subsequent days, the president tweeted that "highly trained, gun adept teachers/coaches would solve the problem instantly, before police arrive" (Merica & Klein, 2018). Police authorities have expressed their concerns and do not support arming adults or students on any campus. The likelihood of innocent people being harmed is greatly increased when untrained, nonpolice authorities carry guns on campus (Stewart, 2018). The National Education Association (NEA) supports the fact that educators need to be focused on educating students, and other solutions that will remove guns from the hands of individuals who intend harm of students in school must be investigated and implemented.

There has been legislation in multiple states regarding firearms on campuses that has been acted upon by state legislatures in 2018. Utah had previously established a law to remove the ability of university presidents or state governing bodies to make regulations regarding carrying concealed weapons on college campuses. Many of the other states have tried to pass legislation that allowed for weapons to be carried by both students and faculty, against the recommendations of police authorities and university and college leaders.

There have been multiple challenges in many states, under constitutional rights and guns on campus (Hinds, 2018). Many of these challenges are impacting the policy discussions for PK–12 schools and guns on campus.

The president appointed the U.S. secretary of education to lead a newly established Federal Commission on School Safety in March 2018. This commission has the responsibility of providing actionable recommendations quickly so that schools are safe learning environments. The other members of this commission include the secretaries of health and human services, homeland security, and the U.S. attorney general. Information is supposed to be gathered over several months from across the country, so that sound recommendations can be made for U.S. schools.

The commission is placing a focus on mental health issues as a major component of consideration (Wermund, 2018). The commission does not seem to be considering research and data that exist from other countries regarding gun control law advocacy. Specifically, information of government intervention to reduce gun access has proven to be effective in other countries. German and Swiss lawmakers quickly responded to mass shootings by changing laws in response to school and other mass shootings. In Switzerland, laws and attitudes toward restricting gun ownership changed after fourteen people were killed in a government entity.

Australia passed the National Firearms Agreement twelve days after a mass shooting, banning automatic and semi-automatic guns for personal use. There have been no school shootings since this occurred in 1996 (Merelli, 2018).

The U.S. Congress has the ability to make change, and the call for change is now. Legal challenges from the NRA and other lobby groups will likely impact the ability of politicians to move quickly, but only because of the political refusal to take on the challenge of the NRA. Many U.S. politicians are financially supported in some way by this group and insist that guns are not the problem. Republicans, who currently control both houses of

Congress, are strong supporters of gun rights in this country. Students from the #NeverAgain movement urge voters to use their political votes and voices to support those lawmakers who support better gun control.

The highly publicized focus on school shootings from February through April 2018 waned by July 2018. In fact, as reported by the *Sandy Hook Promise*, Sen. McConnell, the Senate majority leader, stated that "there's not much Congress can do to prevent school shootings" (Hockley, 2018). Parents of children killed and exposed to school shootings were horrified that this was the response after a few critical months of advocacy and hope.

Public support for better gun control laws grows after each mass shooting event, but within three months following events, it falls back to pre-event levels (Troth & Kahn, 2018). This has been true, as reported by Reuters polls, after each mass shooting in the past decade. Support for firearm restrictions jumped 11 percent after the Sandy Hook shooting, but fell back to the pre-shooting percentage after a three-month period (Troth & Kahn, 2018).

Practitioners need clear, practical plans of action so that they can be prepared in identifying potential problems proactively, respond quickly and appropriately to a crisis, and support all school stakeholders in response to traumatic events in schools. Subsequent chapters of this book provide school and school district leaders with information that can assist them in creating and implementing responsible plans of action and provide tools and resources to deliver those plans of action effectively.

PHYSICAL AND MENTAL HEALTH FACTORS

Issues of mental well-being for students and adults must be considered when discussing school shootings. Often, the perpetrator has issues with mental health. Those impacted who experience a trauma may demonstrate anxiety, stress, and fear, and need mental health professionals to offer practical ways to deal with these factors. While mental health professionals cannot always predict violent actions, there are ways for counselors to assess concerns if they are brought to their attention.

School personnel and students, as well as families of students and community stakeholders, need help in understanding what to look for in their own child or other children. Communication about these issues should be facilitated by individual schools and districts.

Superintendents and school boards struggle to find the right balance to ensure a safe learning environment for all and address the issue of shootings on campuses. Focus needs to be on:

- mental health:
  - proactive signs of students and adults at risk
  - counseling
  - active crisis plans
  - evaluation of implementation
- effective partnerships:
  - police authorities
  - community stakeholders
  - mental health providers
    - medical practitioners
    - psychological support services
    - social agencies
      - counselors
      - crisis intervention
  - facility agents
    - building inspectors
    - fire code inspectors
- parental and family support organizations:
  - PTA/PTOs
  - religious organizations
  - workplace connections
- communication between:
  - police authorities and school leaders
  - school leaders and school employees
  - school employees and each other
  - school employees and community members
  - school employees and parents/families
  - school employees and students

Educators express concern regarding the "numbness" of societal members, as it has been documented that within three months of a tragic event, the expressions of concern and outrage revert back to statistics prior to the event (Reuters, 2018). This statement is one that should concern every member of every community.

The concern about the necessary urgency was expressed by students at a school advisory meeting at a high school in Pasco County, Florida, in June 2018. The school resource officer (SRO) was reporting to this committee of faculty, administrators, parents, community members, and students that the new drill protocols for school worked well during a recent drill. The SRO explained that additional drills would be held over the first six to eight months of the next school year, as school would be ending for the summer in a few weeks. The SRO further explained that the campus had many different entrance and exit points, and future drills would be held from each.

A student said he did not feel safe, and wondered why the drills weren't going to be done from each vantage point as soon as possible. The SRO responded by saying that he would be there, so don't worry. The student, a high school senior, expressed a significant concern that adults were saying things must be done immediately, and then allowing things to occur over time, which made no sense to him. No response was provided.

This is just one example of how communication matters, and what superintendents and other school leaders must think about and discuss with all constituents, including the school board, police authorities, community members, faculty and staff, families, and students. If an issue of safety is a priority, then actions must equal words.

Mental health intervention is critically important to the issues revolving around school safety. In many districts across the United States, the support of school counselors (social workers, psychologists, and guidance counselors) has been deemed "nonmandated services" due to budgetary concerns, and many of those positions have been eliminated, except for mandated services for students with disabilities. This has resulted in a severe lack of preassessment services for students for risk factors dealing with maladaptive behaviors.

In most communities, there is a significant lack of services available to students, and there are long waitlists for those services that do exist. The reality of an adult expressing a concern about a student's mental health and the time it takes for an assessment to occur is a problem in most communities.

In the aftermath of many school shootings, there were signs identified by others of the shooters. There were warning signs, concerns of school personnel, recommendations for mental health intervention, police concern, and so on. The lack of coordinated or sustainable interventions due to a lack of money and other resources indicates the need for resolution.

School leaders need to allocate resources, advocate policy, and develop mechanisms for students, faculty, and staff, by working with school and community stakeholders, and provide services to students who need them. Most communities have agencies that work in areas of mental health support, and collaboration with those agencies could provide needed resources to schools, positively impacting school safety.

This book addresses these issues by identifying concerns and providing ways that schools can be safe learning environments for all. The collaborative work of police authorities, educators, and mental health professionals enables us to see school safety factors from a variety of lenses.

Strategies, consideration of variables, and documented research gives school leaders the information needed to fully address the issues of school safety and provides data to support school and community initiatives to address school shootings comprehensively.

REFERENCES

Ahmed, S., & Walker, C. (2018, May 25). There has been, on average, 1 school shooting every week this year. *CNN*. Retrieved October 26, 2018, from www.cnn. com/2018/03/02/us/school-shootings-2018-list-trnd/index.html.

Alter, C. (2018, March 22). The school shooting generation has had enough. *Time Magazine*.

Ashley, M. (2018, March 14). Guns in schools: It's not just an idea. Here's how some states are already doing it. *USA Today*.

Cowan, K., & Paine, C. (2013, March). School safety: What really works. *Principal Leadership*, 12–15.

Cox, J., & Rich, S. (2018, March 25). Scarred by school safety. *Washington Post*.

Dikel, W. (2012). School shootings and student mental health—What lies beneath the iceberg. Retrieved from www.williamdikel.com.

Grinberg, E., & Muaddi, N. (2018, March 26). How the Parkland students pulled off a massive national protest in only 5 weeks. *CNN*. Retrieved October 26, 2018, from www.cnn.com/2018/03/26/us/march-for-our-lives/index.html.

Hartocollis, A., & Fortin, J. (2018, February 22). Should teachers carry guns? Are metal detectors helpful? What experts say. *New York Times*.

Hinds, T. L. (2018, February 22). 2018 state legislation governing guns on campus. *NASPA*.

Hockley, N. (2018). Senator McConnell calls school shootings "a darn shame." Email from Sandyhookpromise.org. Received July 10, 2018.

Merelli, A. (2018, February 22). Dear America, here's how other countries stop mass shootings. *Quartz*. Retrieved from https://qz.com/1212809/compare-us-mass-shootings-and-gun-control-to-germany-china-russia-switzerland-and-australia.

Merica, D., & Klein, B. (2018). Trump suggests arming teachers as a solution to increase school safety. *CNN*. Retrieved from www.cnn.com/2018/02/21/politics/trump-listening-sessions-parkland-students/index.html.

Troth, D., & Kahn, C. (2018, May 23). Parkland's never again movement didn't really sway gun control. *Reuters*.

Wermund, B. (2018, July 11). Mental health gets top billing at federal safety panel today. *Politico*.

RESOURCES

NASPA Foundation: www.naspa.org/foundation. The NASPA Foundation works to advance the students affairs professions by recognizing achievements, supporting meaningful research and honoring the legacy of NASPA and student affairs leaders, scholars, and practitioners.

National Child Traumatic Stress Network: www.NCTSN.org

National School Board Association: www.nsba.org/services/school-board-leadership-services/school-safety-and-security

Chapter 2

Securing Our Schools

Karin May and Robert Diemer

The environment today has parents and politicians alike scrambling to secure our schools for the future leaders of our country. The recent rash of school shootings has again brought to the forefront a need to investigate avenues to enhance the safety of our schools (Daniels et al., 2010). Although violent crime rates in schools steadily declined during the 1990s, causes of school shootings continue to fuel panic among all. These rare but extremely violent incidents have raised significant questions about the effectiveness of school security measures to warrant the safety of everyone on a school campus (Jennings et al., 2011).

This chapter discusses some simple ways that school design can be used as part of an overall school safety strategy. The techniques presented here have been very beneficial for many schools across the United States, and around the world. It is often little or no cost to utilize them, and they can usually be easily incorporated into new school and renovation projects.

A report was conducted by the U.S. Department of Justice, Federal Bureau of Investigations, and was printed as: *A Study of Active Shooter Incidents in the United States between 2000 and 2013.* In this report, it was found that between 2000 and 2013, there were 160 active shooter incidents in the United States and 1,043 individuals were killed or wounded (U.S. Department of Justice, 2013). Since 2014 to 2017, we have seen an overall increase in these incidents with ninety active shooter incidents occurring between these periods of time (*Statista*, 2017).

The amount of damage that an active shooter can do in a very limited time was demonstrated during the shooting that occurred on the campus of Virginia Polytechnic Institute and State University (VA Tech) in Blacksburg, Virginia, on April 16, 2007. Thirty-two people were killed.

However, as much as we are trying to solve the problem of violence within our schools, there may be a simpler solution that needs no new or revised laws. Law enforcement has a daunting task for protecting society, utilizing a large net approach. With the onset of foreign and domestic terrorism, and gang and street violence, law enforcement—like firefighters—seem to be putting out the proverbial fires with little or no extra support. After the seventeen lives lost in the February 14, 2018, Parkland school shooting, lawmakers in Florida passed a law expecting every public school to have a security officer in place.

Nevertheless, they have at their disposal a finite supply of additional help with a little investment, and each year some of that investment (officers) leaves full-time work to take on the life of retirement. In the Tampa Bay region it was mandated that every school have an armed officer by July 1, 2018. The issue that law enforcement, school districts, and county governments are encountering is sticker shock of the state mandate. In the state of New Jersey, putting armed guards inside schools was, virtually, an unprecedented concept just over ten years ago. Today, the demand for stronger security is a crucial part of school budgets.

A new law in New Jersey is aimed at giving districts another resource, the ability to hire specially trained, retired police officers for security at public and private schools and on community college campuses. The concept that should be considered is expanding and, in some cases, developing a reserve or part-time law enforcement program. In Florida, the school safety officers, school protection officers (SPOs), and school safety guardian would cost about $2.1 million to implement, without including training of 132 hours per person. The assigned officers will be accountable for working with the district's Safe Schools division to provide security to our campuses, conduct necessary drills, oversee crime prevention initiatives and programs with students, conduct surveillance, and other security-related tasks.

The idea is that many retired officers would volunteer their time to continue their service to the public. It is the notion that agencies could put additional officers to supplement or even assist the School Resource Officer Program, which adds another layer of protection within our educational intuitions and to improve relations between police and youth (Lambert & McGinty, 2002). In Israel, most terror attacks are stopped by armed civilians, not law enforcement. This approach, along with incorporating the concept of *crime prevention through environmental design* (CPTED), would not require agencies to deplete other areas to *protect and serve.*

CPTED is a comparatively new concept. The goal of CPTED is the reduction of occasions for crime to occur, and in this case, prevent any further violence in our educational institutions. The importance of providing effective active shooter training to individuals impacted by an act of violence or other crisis in school settings cannot be overstated (Crepeau-Hobson & Summers, 2011).

Today, more than ever, we have observed an increase in school violence. The notion of sending our children to school to become productive members of society is overshadowed by news reports of mass shootings within our educational institutions. The situation at Columbine High School, Littleton, Colorado, started cascading changes within law enforcement, on responding to an active shooter. Columbine did not occur in isolation, but instead, was the most serious of a cluster of seven school shootings occurring within a nineteen-month period (Kleck, 2009). As early as the nineteenth century, schools in America began planning for school emergencies.

For instance, in Bath County, Michigan, a school bombing in 1972 killed nearly three times the number of victims as the Columbine High School massacre. These shootings would become a familiar pattern. Many individuals that target school settings do not plan on surviving the attack. Even this tragedy, basically forgotten, represents the extreme example of school mass murder.

According to the Federal Bureau of Investigations (FBI), an active shooter is defined as "an individual actively engaged in killing or attempting to kill people in a populated area" (U.S. Department of Justice, 2018). More and more, each day, month, and year, since April 20, 1999, school administrators, educators, police, and politicians have been all trying to construct a policy and response that not only reduce violence levels in schools but also increase the response time to neutralize the circumstances. School emergency plans have evolved significantly. These plans are driven by federal and state authorities and have a significant level of complexity.

The emergency plan response would require cooperation from the school administration and local police officials. Regardless of how ineffective some policies might appear in the light of mass school killings that do occur, those same policies might have short-circuited still other violent events that never came to be (Kleck, 2009).

One measure that the state of Florida has taken after the Marjory Stoneman Douglas High School shooting in Parkland, Florida, where three educators and fourteen students were killed, is to pass legislation that requires anyone purchasing a gun to be twenty-one years of age and have a three-day waiting period to take custody of it. The Marjory Stoneman Douglas High School Public Safety Act outlines substantial reforms to make schools in Florida safer while keeping firearms out of the reach of mentally ill and dangerous individuals. It also charges the Florida Department of Education with producing the Office of Safe Schools, which will offer regulation with best practices in school security, threat assessments, and emergency preparedness, to name a few.

The Safe School Initiative suggests that some future attacks may be preventable and recommends the use of a threat assessment approach as a promising strategy for preventing school shootings. While threat assessment shows some promise, it is basically the concept of carefully investigating and evaluating every possible threat (Stanley, 1996). Currently, to acquire a handgun in Florida from a licensed firearm dealer you must be twenty-one years of age, or eighteen to purchase a handgun from a private citizen, but if you want to purchase a rifle or shotgun, you only need to be eighteen. In Vermont, they have imposed new restrictions for gun ownership that require new background checks, restrict purchase age to twenty-one, and ban bumpstock weapons and large-capacity ammunition clips.

As reported by the Pew Charitable Trusts, "In the two weeks since the Florida school massacre, state lawmakers around the country have introduced bills to ban bump stocks, ban assault weapons, and expand background check—and also to arm teachers, lighten penalties for carrying without a permit, and waive handgun permit fees" (Vasilogambors, 2018).

During the past ten years, a tremendous variety of school safety programs and strategies have been implemented, including programs such as "zero tolerance" and the use of cameras and metal detection devices, to name a few (Lambert & McGinty, 2002). The law enforcement community has also been active in developing programs to help stop school violence. One program is RUN. HIDE. FIGHT.® According to _Psychology Today_, by 2014, there were "nearly three million YouTube Views" on this video and program (Albrecht, 2014). The concept was birthed by the City of Houston, Texas, along with the Department of Homeland Security (DHS).

The concept is plain and simple; RUN—avoid an assailant by getting out of the structure safely by running as fast as you can if it is safe to do so. If this is not possible, and you must stay, then, HIDE—get to a safe room, or a location where you can barricade yourself inside. Silence your phone, don't make any noise, and don't come out until receiving an alert from a law enforcement officer to do so. However, if you are found, and there is no place to go, FIGHT—it may be necessary to fight to improve your chances of surviving. Do not be passive. Take assertive action by fighting back with whatever you can find. This safety campaign has been presented to workers, law enforcement, colleges/universities, and others as the first step in training to act and preventing loss of life.

The Department of Justice's Bureau of Justice Assistance along with the FBI and Texas State University's Advanced Law Enforcement Rapid Response Training (ALERRT) Center, created a program for the first responders arriving at an active shooting situation (Texas State University, 2018). This training has been provided to over 114,000 law enforcement officers and has been adopted by police agencies throughout the United States as the national standard response protocol.

Further, to ensure that the first responders are prepared, police agencies have now mandated training on how to stop bleeding from gunshot wounds. To date, most police agencies have been provided with little to no medical training outside of the first aid and CPR requirements. With the onslaught of shooting incidents, the American College of Surgeons developed a program, *Stop the Bleed*. The program is designed for the first responder—generally, law enforcement officers—to be able to assist shooting victims with gunshot wounds. Past incidents have shown that high-powered weapons have the capability of severing major limbs or cause massive injuries and holes in the body.

Many victims of an active shooter have succumbed to their wounds as they have bled out. The training identifies the proper use of a tourniquet on the arms or legs, as well as the packing of the injuries to control the bleeding. In addition to the training, agencies are providing responders small medical kits that include a tourniquet, bandages, and clotting materials.

SECURITY/POLICE AT EDUCATIONAL INSTITUTIONS

To act quickly and ease society's stress about school shootings, the law enforcement community has been put into a situation where they are moving to arm the schools with uniform police or security officers. Part of the reason is for the general public to have restored faith that local law enforcement understands the fears and are the ones responsible for protecting society. However, after the terrorist situations that faced America on September 11, 2001, the flying public was nervous, causing a host of problems. The government utilized the National Guard throughout the United States to supplement the policing efforts by having guardsman assigned to the various airports.

No matter how noble it was, most realized that it reduced fear and allowed people to go about their routine duties. The idea of the military in the airport did serve as a deterrent to criminal actions, but it also provided a sense of security. The placing of armed police/security at the schools will also have the same effect—however, at a substantial cost. How agencies respond to this differs significantly. Some police agencies may reduce their patrol resources in the community to have officers at the school. This method can influence response times and overall effect on crime. Several law enforcement agencies in the greater Tampa Bay area in Florida are looking at hiring armed uniformed security officers.

These security officers would augment the school resource officer or just be placed in a school on their own. In Largo, Florida, the police department is hiring part-time police officers, in uniform, to work at the schools. These officers are provided a salary, with no benefits, and the officers only work the days school is in session. These and many other ideas are being discussed. However, most have a significant monetary impact on the community in which they serve.

There is one concept that may have been overlooked. Each year, hundreds of law enforcement officers retire from local, county, state, or federal agencies. These retirees settle into communities, and many seek out police reserve positions. Police reserves are sworn officers and typically work with an agency to augment services; many do not receive salaries nor benefits. The reason they serve is to volunteer in a career they loved and to remain a sworn law enforcement officer within the state.

Using this concept, police agencies could expand the reserve program and use those officers to fulfill the authority presence at a school or educational institution. The price of the program is much lower than many others, and the concept would be incredibly appealing to the volunteers. Whatever is decided, it is safe to assume that in the years to come, students will see a more visible presence of police on their campuses. The presence of police/security will be much differently defined than the current school resource officer program but will have a significant visual appeal for safety and security of those present.

CRIME PREVENTION THROUGH ENVIRONMENTAL DESIGN (CPTED)

The CPTED program was instituted in the 1970s and was developed to look at reducing crime by using the environment and constructional designs. The program has three principles that guide the entire process: natural access control, natural surveillance, and territorial reinforcement. Many law enforcement agencies enacted crime prevention units where police officers would teach the public about the concept of target hardening. Education and law enforcement officials have begun to take serious action toward preventing school crime and educating their students and faculty about violence in school through target hardening (Jennings et al., 2011).

For instance, locks, video cameras, alarm security systems, panic buttons, and fortified windows were just a few of the items that could assist with bunkering down a residence or building (Krehnke, 2015). Ideally, the classroom doors should have a significant ability to resist forced entry if a room is to be used as a shelter-in-place plan. The state of New York alone spent over $28 million on metal detectors to assist in the reduction of guns and knives on school premises (Jennings et al., 2011). Metal detectors may have some utility deterring routine daily carrying of weapons into schools, but they are not relevant to premeditated acts of mass violence (Kleck, 2009).

The goal of CPTED begins at the design process stage, looking at the space, design, and use of a location. However, the CPTED model incorporated the target-hardening aspect in the early design, but it was later incorporated into the three principles. What the proponents of CPTED found was that target hardening frequently came after a crime incident had occurred. These principles were not sought after right from the beginning.

The CPTED model is simplistic in its concept and takes in some very straightforward processes. Let's look at Target department stores. If you have ever seen one, you will notice right away the large, red, ball-shaped, concrete fixtures that are strategically placed in front of the store's entrances. These concrete fixtures are referred to as *bollards*. Many Target stores have eight evenly placed across the entrance. If the placement was done by intention or not, you could look at it as part of the CPTED model. The bollards are made of concrete and are spaced evenly in front of the doors (Figure 2.1).

Figure 2.1.

These bollards are also seen throughout Israel to prevent vehicles from driving into structures. The use of bollards helps to reduce negative visual impact and are pleasant to look at, yet they constitute a significant security component without resorting to the prison camp approach to security. The construction of the bollards helps to prevent or reduce the effects of a vehicle smashing through the doors of a store or a crowd of people. These devices are more prevalent than you may realize. Many similar devices are affixed outside convenience stores also to mitigate damages and injuries.

If you look at government buildings, you will see physical concrete barriers used as a traffic management device. In some cases, they look like large flowerpots or other unnoticeable items. However, they are there to discourage crime. Fencing is also considered a form of CPTED. There is no escaping the fact that physical security has some significant limitations. Schools by their nature are public, high-traffic environments, so any physical security measures must be adjusted to accommodate those conditions.

Physical security must be designed to be reasonably low cost and user-friendly if schools are expected to implement them. As an element of physical security, fencing is not intended to create an impenetrable fortress, but to make penetration more difficult. The advantage of fencing in an educational institution provides safety-related benefits—for example, enhancing privacy, controlling access to one way in and one way out, and depending on the type of fencing, protection from bullets.

Fencing is one idea we can take from Israel. Almost every school in Israel is fenced in. To gain entrance to a school, everyone must pass through an arm-guarded locked gate, requiring a set of questions to be answered and proper identification given. There has recently been a trend in Australia toward the use of high-security fencing around the entire school grounds. The security is standard and represents how school grounds in Australia are secured (Rooney, 2015). The concept of CPTED is an approach that is used by planners, architects, security officials, and citizens to be proactive against crime.

Natural Access Control

The concept of natural access control looks at decreasing the opportunity for crime to be committed. Adequately located entrances, exits, landscaping, and lighting can subtly direct foot traffic and vehicles and may decrease criminal activity (Figure 2.2). For example, a business may have full windows that are not obscured so that people can see into the location without obstruction. Limited access to the site, which does not restrict the flow of individuals, limits escape routes or makes it difficult to navigate quickly. The idea is to make the perpetrator feel uncomfortable about committing the crime.

Figure 2.2.

Natural Surveillance

The concept of natural surveillance is to keep the criminal under observation. For example, when an individual is contemplating committing a crime, they perceive that they are being watched. Natural surveillance can also include the ability for people to hear one another to help prevent criminal activity. Doing this requires the use of small plants or shrubs that would not allow a person to hide, open walkways that are not covered and allow for long-term visibility, and the use of curbing to direct movement of individuals to keep them on a particular path.

Territorial Reinforcement

The last concept looks at individual responsibility, where an individual takes ownership of the space and is willing to challenge anyone or anything that abuses the space or is unwanted. Individuals naturally want to protect a territory they feel is their own. Territorial reinforcement is when a person takes responsibility to ensure the areas are clear and free of debris and provides maintenance when necessary. Boundaries between public and restricted

Figure 2.3.

areas can be achieved by using physical elements such as fences, signs, and landscaping (Figure 2.3). These are ways to assist in the identification of intruders. Territorial reinforcement can be seen to work when space is created to discourage potential offenders (Crowe, 2003).

CPTED AND SCHOOLS

Now that we have looked at the various methods to reduce violence, the belief is that we use all of this to reinforce our schools. The theory would look at building a safe school. Today, more than ever, school administrators and planners need to reevaluate the current structure of the school. One must look at the physical location first, starting with the outside. Schools need to conform to the CPTED program by removing trees, bushes, or other barriers that obstruct school windows, to avoid anyone hiding.

On the outside, entirely around the school, should be fencing that makes it very difficult for a person to climb, and if they did, they would probably be seen. The fencing must completely encompass the entire campus with locked gated access to open areas. The fences must be back far enough so that an individual would be visible if they were able to scale or get under the fence and move toward the structures. This fencing would be the first line of defense to the school.

Natural access control can assist staff members and school administrators to control a campus by creating boundaries within public and private places and help with guiding people to designated areas. Well-designed front entryways can allow staff to control access remotely. These areas also typically require either natural surveillance or visibility using or installing and monitoring closed-circuit television video cameras or reflected mirrors, as well as techniques for staff to speak to visiting individuals, such as a glass window or an intercom system.

Architectural designs that enhance natural surveillance (such as glass office windows) and the use of high counters can improve the security of the front office. One important aspect of natural access control to remember is, although these strategies may limit the opportunity for crimes, they should not hinder the mobility of potential victims.

By working from the perimeter into the center of the school, barriers would need to be installed that do not detract from the look of a school but that prevent vehicles from leaving the roadway and slamming into a crowd of students. This prevention would require the installation of pipe bollards along with walkways that separate the students from the thoroughfares. The bollards would also serve another purpose of clearly defining the walkway areas and redirecting individuals to only the limited access points to gain entrance to the designated corridors.

The administration would then have to look at all the entries into the structures and consider the concept of a closed campus. Taking exit/entrance doors and moving them to emergency exits only would have a profound effect in directing student movement. The interior of the doors would have to have the locking mechanisms similar to the airport emergency exits onto the tarmac. These doors have a push bar that will open within a few seconds but only after emitting an alarm. The doors would dramatically reduce the chance of anyone exiting during a nonemergency event and prevent a quick escape of an offender.

Following that idea, the next area would be where all students and visitors would have to enter the building. There is significant variation in school construction with older schools constructed differently than more modern schools. However, it would be possible to identify the most common types of wall and door installation and test their ability to resist forced entry and their ballistic resistance. Limiting the access to one entrance, where staff and security can monitor it, would reduce the potential of having someone access the property without being noticed.

The single entrance concept intentionally makes a funnel or choking point for all activity, which is a deterrent in and of itself. It is here that schools may employ metal detectors or police/security personnel to have a visible deterrent. As previously mentioned, this area should have high counters reinforced to protect the staff or personnel from a stray bullet or projectile. The entrances and exits must be unobstructed to allow a steady flow of uninterrupted personnel. Since congestion could occur at the end of school, another area for students to exit the facility could be opened for a mass exodus.

As the exterior has been improved, so must the interior. All interior doors should have locking mechanisms that allow individuals to shelter in place. Closed-circuit cameras should be installed in all hallways so that at any one given time, individuals can monitor all movement activity throughout the entire campus. Emergency bandage packs can be strategically placed in the halls, similar to the placement of automated external defibrillators (AED) that are visible in public areas. This allows for immediate response with bandages to stop bleeding for wounded individuals.

Once the inside is adequately outfitted, the administration must look at nonstructural areas to provide protection. One such area is school uniforms. Wearing school uniforms at school not only confirms a smaller chance of violence but also helps in creating a healthy team culture and harmony on campus. The concept of uniforms has so many benefits, including reducing the wearing of gang clothing, and is a subtle way for improving natural surveillance. The instantaneous value comes in when a person enters the campus in street clothes, as they stand out from everyone else and are easily recognized as an intruder or a nonstudent.

Troubled students at any school benefit a great deal from this team culture. Usually, such students are known to isolate themselves and keep their motives and feelings to themselves. These troubled students become self-centered and may cause issues at home and school. Often these are the students that become prime targets for bullying.

Parents want reinsurance that when they send their children to school, they are going to be safe from danger. Studies have shown that the rate of assaults, fighting, injuries, and attacks with a deadly weapon decreased by 50 percent after schools changed their policy from casual dress to school uniforms (Wade & Stafford, 2003).

The last measure, which is equally as important as all the other areas mentioned, is training. Today, many companies and government organizations have produced school training programs for staff and students. The Department of Homeland Security has prepared online training to address the needs of those in active shooter situations (Department of Homeland Security, n.d.). The training is an essential element to ensure that all persons, including students, teachers, staff, and visitors, know how to react in the event of a situation like this.

In addition to confronting individuals who seem to not fit in a situation, many private companies are also working behind the scenes to add security to educational institutions. The body-worn camera systems that are utilized by police are now being introduced for those providing individuals protection within the school systems. The concept is to be an added layer to prevent criminal acts, by notifying individuals that they may be filmed. The visible body-worn camera system acts as a visual deterrence.

Some of the modifications require financial support. It is the responsibility of the school administrators, police, politicians, and, most of all, parents, guardians, and family members of the students to take the responsibility to improve the physical barriers and become involved. Involvement can also be in the form of volunteering to patrol or be present in the school or the school-yard as a visual deterrence.

SCHOOL SAFETY CHECKLIST

As school administrators are seeking innovative ways to secure their educational institutions, the U.S. Department of Homeland Security has developed a School Violence Prevention and Intervention Checklist that will allow administrators to evaluate their institution. The checklist is not all-inclusive; however, it does provide the reviewer with an overall understanding of their capabilities. In addition, the results can be used to ether improve the security or as a document to strengthen students' and parents' understanding of the security measures in place (Department of Homeland Security, n.d.).

School Violence Prevention and Intervention Checklist

Use the following checklist to assess the school's current level of safety related to prevention and intervention efforts (Table 2.1). If an element is in place, check "Yes." If changes need to be made, check "Improve." If the element is not in place, check "No."

GEORGIA SCHOOL SAFETY ASSESSMENT

In March of 2018, the Georgia Department of Education developed a compressive School Safety Assessment that incorporated the CPTED model of security protection along with a checklist for administrative procedures. This checklist is extensive and can be modified for the educational situation of most systems (Georgia Department of Education, 2018).

Table 2.1.

	Implement	Improve	Yes	No	N/A
1. Students have access to conflict-resolution programs.					
2. Students are assisted in developing anger-management skills.					
3. Prevention of harassment is emphasized school wide.					
4. Bilingual and multicultural resources are available to students and staff members.					
5. Programs are available for students who are academically at risk.					
6. Students may ask for help without the loss of confidentiality.					
7. Students and parents are aware of community resources.					
8. A bully prevention program is in place.					
9. The school has a well-developed network of service providers to which students can be referred.					
10. Crisis prevention is an integral part of the school's safety plan—that is, practice of emergency drills and evacuation, a partnership with law enforcement officials, metal detection capability, and adequate adult monitoring at all times.					
11. Adequate suicide-prevention support systems are in place for students.					
12. The school has implemented a character education program in accordance with the state code.					

This checklist was modified from School Safety Assessment Protocol, Virginia Department of Education (www.sedl.org/secac/pdfs/safetyassessment.pdf).

Components of the School Safety Assessment

The level of safety in a school must be assessed using multiple indicators that apply to the total school environment. At a minimum, the assessment process will address the following:

- safety and security of buildings and grounds
- school procedures/guidelines
- offenses/consequences outlined in the Student Code of Conduct
- role of law enforcement/school resource officer (SRO)
- mandatory reporting of criminal activity to law enforcement
- review of the emergency/crisis school safety plan
- administrative procedures
- staff development opportunities concerning safety and legal responsibilities
- federal laws concerning students with disabilities
- procedures for data collection
- review of current discipline data
- prevention/intervention/student support plans
- opportunities for student involvement
- opportunities for parent involvement
- school climate surveys

Assessment Data Sources

Table 2.2.

Safe and Orderly Environment	Robert J. Marzano What Works in Schools: Translating Research into Action
Safe and Orderly Schools	National Association of Secondary School Principals
Best Practices for School Safety	Georgia Emergency Management Agency (GEMA)
	Georgia Department of Education (GaDOE)
	Virginia Department of Education

Assessment Information

Table 2.3: Building and Grounds Checklist

A. *School Interior*	Yes	No	N/A
1. The designated entrance door has clearly visible signs showing the location of the main office and advising visitors to report to the office.			
2. The entrance lobby is visible from the main office.			
3. Staff members, volunteer personnel, or a security camera monitor the main entrance lobby.			
4. Visitors are required to sign in and out at the main office.			
5. Hallways are free of travel impediments.			
6. Hallways leading to required exit doors are kept clear and unencumbered with rugs or furniture, which might impede traffic flow from building.			
7. Blind spots in hallways and stairwells are equipped with parabolic mirrors (or a similar surveillance device).			
8. Remote and isolated hallways are monitored by security cameras or other monitoring methods.			
9. Stairwells are monitored.			
10. Restrooms are inspected for cleanliness and safety on a regular basis.			
11. Restroom walls and stalls are free of graffiti.			
12. Restrooms have a smoke detector.			
13. Restrooms comply with ADA requirements.			
14. All cafeteria food and perishables are stored properly.			
15. Choking guidelines are clearly posted in cafeteria dining area.			
16. Cafeteria staff can hear school alarms and announcements.			
17. A staff member is assigned to make sure the cafeteria staff is contacted in the event of a lockdown or severe weather threat.			
18. Surveillance cameras and monitors are installed in strategic locations.			
19. If a classroom is vacant, students are restricted from entering unsupervised.			
20. Classroom doors remain closed and locked when classes are in session.			
21. Seating for the disabled is available, as per ADA requirements, in the auditorium and the gym.			

22. Clear and precise emergency evacuation routes are posted at critical locations.			
23. Fire extinguisher locations are clearly marked and regularly inspected.			
24. School staff is trained on the use of fire extinguishers.			
25. Access to catwalk and prop areas is restricted.			
26. Access to electrical panels is restricted.			
B. Lighting	Yes	No	N/A
1. The main lobby is properly lighted.			
2. The hallways are properly lighted.			
3. Bathrooms are properly lighted.			
4. Classrooms are properly lighted.			
5. Hallways have emergency lighting.			
6. Emergency lighting is in working condition.			
7. Exit signs are properly lighted, clearly visible, and point in the correct exit direction.			
C. Doors	Yes	No	N/A
1. Faculty members are required to lock classrooms upon leaving.			
2. Exterior doors into the building remain locked at all times and include signage advising visitors to report to the main office.			
3. Doors accessing internal courtyards are locked to prevent outside entry.			
4. Areas accessible to intruders are secure.			
5. All doors are properly labeled and numbered.			
6. Cafeteria service delivery door remains locked at all times.			
D. Lab Safety/Chemicals/Hazardous Storage	Yes	No	N/A
1. Boiler room is clean, is free of debris, is not used for storage, access is controlled, and is inspected.			
2. Lab safety procedures are reviewed and clearly posted.			
3. Chemicals are securely locked when not in use.			
4. Lab preparation areas, hazardous storage areas, and mechanical rooms are properly protected from unauthorized access.			
5. Science labs are equipped with a fire extinguisher and a fire blanket.			
6. Eye wash stations in labs and vocational shops are in working condition.			

(Continued)

Table 2.3: (Continued)

7. Hazardous objects (knives, scalpels, tools, etc.) are securely locked when not in use.			
8. Chemical storage areas are locked and cleaned, and a Material Safety Data Sheet (MSDS) contains information regarding the proper procedures for handling, storing, and disposing of chemical substances.			
9. An MSDS accompanies all chemicals or kits that contain chemicals.			
10. All MSDSs are saved and stored in a designated file or binder using a system that is organized and easy to understand.			
11. MSDS collection is placed in a central, easily accessible location known to all workers and emergency personnel.			
12. Paint booths, auto shops, and welding booths are well ventilated and exhaust directly to the exterior.			

School Exterior

E. Signage	Yes	No	N/A
1. Visitor signs are posted near entrance advising visitors to report to the main office.			
2. Weapons law signs are clearly posted at the main entrance.			
3. Drug-free/tobacco-free campus signs are posted.			
4. Visitor and handicapped parking areas are clearly marked.			

F. Extracurricular/Play Areas	Yes	No	N/A
1. Emergency vehicles can access play and athletic fields easily.			
2. Bleachers are in good condition (no signs of rust).			
3. The risers between bleacher seats are protected to prevent entrapment and children from falling through.			
4. Field houses can be secured for safety and security.			
5. The school ground is free of obstacles, graffiti, trash, and debris.			
6. Surveillance cameras are installed in strategic locations.			
7. Stadium evacuation procedures are posted.			
8. Mechanical, electrical, and other equipment on school grounds are surrounded by a protective enclosure.			
9. Deep recesses in buildings with wings are fenced for safety.			

G. Surveillance	Yes	No	N/A
1. The school has designated points of entry that are monitored to control building access.			

2. Visual surveillance of parking lots or monitoring by remote security cameras is possible from the main office or some other area.			
3. The location of trailers/portable classrooms enables natural surveillance.			
4. If located in isolated areas, the trailers/portable classrooms are monitored with security cameras.			
5. Trailers/portable classrooms are connected to the school's central alarm system.			
6. Crawl spaces below building/trailers/portable classrooms are closed off.			
7. Shrubbery and trees are well trimmed.			
8. Law enforcement, security, or other staff members patrol parking areas during school hours.			
9. Student drivers and staff members must obtain parking decals or some other appropriate form of identification to authorize legitimate parking on school property.			
H. Lighting	**Yes**	**No**	**N/A**
1. There is adequate lighting around the building to enhance night safety.			
2. Lighting is provided at the entrances and other points of possible intrusion.			
3. There is adequate lighting around trailers/portable classrooms.			
4. Directional lights are aimed at the building.			
5. Lighting in the parking lot provides uniform coverage to support camera surveillance.			
I. Windows and Doors	**Yes**	**No**	**N/A**
1. Windows and doors are in good repair.			
2. Windows and doors are adequately secured after hours.			
3. Building perimeter is free from trees, branches, and telephone poles that may provide unauthorized access to upper floor levels or roof.			
4. All exterior doors have non-removable hinge pins.			
5. Exterior doors, unless designated for entry, have no exterior hardware.			
6. Exterior double doors have an astragal (plate) covering the gap between doors.			
7. Required exit doors are equipped with panic hardware.			

(Continued)

Table 2.3: (Continued)

8. Doors accessing internal courtyards are tied into the central alarm system.			
9. The school has developed written regulations regarding access to and use of the building by school personnel after regular school hours.			
J. Student Transportation Issues	**Yes**	**No**	**N/A**
1. Staff members check bus loading/unloading area and pick-up/drop-off area before vehicles arrive to identify any possible hazards or impediments, and to make certain no unauthorized persons or vehicles are in the area.			
2. Staff members are assigned to bus area during loading/unloading and the staff members understand their responsibilities for reporting any problems.			
3. Access to bus loading/unloading areas is restricted during arrival/dismissal.			
4. An area is designated as the pick-up/drop-off zone for non–bus riders and is supervised by assigned staff members.			
5. An emergency dismissal procedure is in place (i.e., student and staff evacuation from facility and vicinity).			
School Procedures/Guidelines			
K. Security	**Yes**	**No**	**N/A**
1. School has a procedure for handling all cash collected.			
2. An escort is available for school personnel responsible for money collected or deposited during the school day.			
3. Unused areas of the school can be closed off during after-school activities.			
4. Two-way communication is possible between administrators and SROs.			
5. Teachers have the capability of communicating to the office from their classrooms.			
6. There is a central alarm system.			
7. Alarm system is tested on a regular basis.			
8. Photo identification badges are issued to all employees (including support staff and bus drivers) and are clearly visible.			
9. Visitors are required to sign in and out.			
10. Visitor/guest badges are issued.			
11. Proper photo ID is required of vendors, repairmen, etc.			

12. **One person is designated to perform the following security checks at the end of each day:**			
• Check that all classrooms and offices are locked.			
• Check all classrooms, restrooms, locker rooms, and other school areas to ensure that everyone has left the building.			
• Check all exterior entrances to ensure that they are locked.			
• Check the security alarm system.			
L. Law Enforcement Role	Yes	No	N/A
1. A School Resource Officer is assigned to the school.			
2. Law enforcement monitors school grounds after regular school hours and can contact school administrator(s).			
3. Incidents of crime that occur on school property/events are reported to law enforcement and other appropriate agencies.			
4. Law enforcement personnel are involved in the development of the school safety plan.			
5. The school and law enforcement have an agreement of understanding that clearly defines the roles and responsibilities of each group.			
M. Emergency/Crisis Plan	Yes	No	N/A
1. The school has an Emergency/Crisis Plan.			
2. Local law enforcement and first responders were consulted in the development of the plan.			
3. The plan includes all categories as required by state law.			
4. The plan is reviewed and updated each year.			
5. The staff has received training on emergency procedures.			
6. The staff has access to the Emergency/Crisis Plan.			
7. The plan has been submitted to GEMA.			
8. The plan includes clear strategies for dealing with the media in the event of a crisis.			
9. The plan includes a component for post-crisis response, such as the availability of counseling services for students and staff members, dealing with the probability of "copycat" incidents, and dealing with post-traumatic stress.			
10. Primary and secondary evacuation sites have been predetermined for fires (500 feet) and bomb threats (1000 feet).			
11. School has developed an evacuation plan to accommodate students and staff with physical disabilities in the event of a crisis.			

(Continued)

Table 2.3: (Continued)

12. Tabletop exercises and/or practices have been conducted with staff.			
13. A reunification site has been established in case of emergency evacuation.			
14. School staff is aware of proper response to blood and body fluid spills.			
15. An appropriate number of staff members are trained in CPR.			
16. School has access to an AED/defibrillator.			
17. An appropriate number of staff members are trained in the use of AED/defibrillator.			
18. Fire drills/tornado drills are conducted as required by state law.			
19. Fire drills are reported to the Office of Insurance and Safety Fire Commissioner in a timely manner.			
20. The school maintains a record of fire inspection by the local or state fire officer.			
21. School has a sprinkler system installed for fire suppression.			
22. Intruder alert drills are conducted.			
23. Intruder alert procedures are in place to inform bus drivers on field trips to delay returning to the school until the "all clear" signal is given.			
24. School has a pandemic/epidemic preparedness plan.			
25. School has carbon monoxide detectors.			
26. School has a backup generator on site for use in power outages			
27. School has a procedure for securing students during an intruder alert who are on the playground or athletic fields, in locker rooms, in the gymnasium, and/or in the cafeteria.			
N. Administrative Procedures	Yes	No	N/A
1. School or school district conducts pre-employment background checks for all employees.			
2. The principal and administrative staff are highly visible.			
3. The Student Code of Conduct is revised and reviewed annually (students/staff).			
4. Students and/or parents sign for receipt of Student Code of Conduct.			
5. Behavioral expectations and consequences for violations are clearly outlined.			
6. A chain of command has been established when the principal is away.			

7. Disciplinary consequences are fairly and consistently enforced.			
8. Security measures/administrative supervision is established for extracurricular activities.			
9. Staff members are assigned to supervise students (halls/bus/restrooms/cafeteria).			
10. Parents are an integral part of the planning of student discipline procedures and actions.			
11. Student medicines are secured (locked cabinet/desk).			
12. Student checkout procedures are in place (only to an authorized adult).			
13. Teachers/administrators are aware of mandatory reporting requirements (weapons, drugs, child abuse, etc.).			
14. Federal/state laws regarding students with disabilities are followed.			
15. Policies and procedures have been developed to allow students to transfer to another school if they are a victim of a violent criminal offense.			
16. School files and records are maintained in locked, fireproof containers or vaults.			
17. There is a control system in place to monitor keys and duplicates and/or card access systems.			
18. School maintains a record of required health permits.			
19. A log is maintained of all chemicals and other dangerous substances.			
20. The school maintains records of all maintenance on doors, windows, lockers, and other areas of the school.			
21. All field trips have a manifest on the school bus and at the school. In the event of an emergency, it is essential to account for all students, faculty, and volunteers.			
O. Data Collection and Reporting	**Yes**	**No**	**N/A**
1. An incident-reporting database has been established.			
2. Discipline incidents are accurately recorded as required by law.			
3. The school has established a system for analyzing data to identify recurring problems and to provide information relative to prevention and intervention procedures.			
4. The school has developed a procedure for periodic review and update of the incident-reporting system.			
5. Discipline incidents are regularly monitored.			

(Continued)

Table 2.3: (Continued)

6. Administrators are aware of mandatory reporting requirements (weapons, drugs, child abuse, etc.).			
7. Chronic discipline procedures have been developed concerning students with recurring problems.			
8. Students are referred to a disciplinary tribunal hearing for serious violations of school rules.			
9. The outcome of disciplinary tribunal hearings is recorded in the student's discipline record.			
10. Unsafe School Choice Option (USCO) violations are accurately reported in the end-of-year data-collection process.			
11. School staff has been trained to accurately report USCO violations and discipline incidents on the annual discipline report.			
P. Prevention and Intervention	Yes	No	N/A
1. Bullying prevention programs or strategies are in place.			
2. Students have access to conflict-resolution/peer-mediation programs.			
3. Students may ask for help without the loss of confidentiality.			
4. School policy provides a system whereby staff and students may report problems, incidents, or potential dangers anonymously.			
5. Diversity awareness is emphasized.			
6. Academic programs are available for "at-risk students."			
7. Students and parents are aware of school student support resources.			
8. School has a well-developed network of service providers to which students can be referred.			
9. Adequate suicide-prevention support systems are in place for students.			
10. Administrators and teachers have been trained to recognize the early warning signs of potentially suicidal students, including knowledge of the appropriate steps in referring students for help.			
11. Counselors facilitate student assistance programs/groups.			
12. Students have opportunities to be actively involved.			
13. Parents are encouraged to volunteer and play an active role in the school.			
14. School has implemented a character education program in accordance with state law.			
15. School safety and violence prevention information is provided regularly to staff as part of a school or system-wide staff development plan.			

As administrators are securing schools to prevent or discourage violence, police and emergency personnel are working to decrease response times to incidents. At the school shooting at Columbine High School, we saw officers respond and set up the perimeter and wait for the Special Weapons and Tactics (SWAT) team to arrive to confront the suspects. This delay caused the unfortunate loss of more lives. Due to this, police have redefined today's policy where officers do not wait to enter into hot zones (areas where hostile activity is taking place) and are now trained to enter immediately and search out the offender.

Between 2016 and 2018, there has been a paradigm shift in policy, where police and rescue personnel are now joining to enter into warm zones (safer areas than a hot zone) to attend to the victims. This model is known as the Rescue Task Force (RTF) concept. After the shooter is either captured, killed, or barricaded, the RTF will go into action. Police officers along with medical personnel enter the warm zone to attend to those wounded individuals. This allows emergency rescue workers to put hands on as many people as possible, treating those with life-threatening injuries to reduce deaths. The tactical change in officer response, now coupled with the RTF concept, has reduced the loss of life.

REFERENCES

Albrecht, S. (2014). The truth behind the Run-Hide-Fight debate. *Psychology Today*. Retrieved May 25, 2018, from www.fbi.gov/about/partnerships/office-of-partner-engagement/active-shooter-resources.

Crepeau-Hobson, F., & Summers, L. L. (2011). The crisis response to a school-based hostage event: A case study. *Journal of School Violence*, *10*(3), 281–298. doi:10.1080/15388220.2011.578277

Daniels, J., Volungis, A., Pshenishny, E., Gandhi, P., Winkler, A., Cramer, D., & Bradley, M. (2010). A qualitative investigation of averted school shooting rampages. *The Counseling Psychologist*, *38*(1), 69–95.

Department of Homeland Security. (2018). Active shooter preparedness. Retrieved from www.dhs.gov/active-shooter-preparedness.

Department of Homeland Security. (n.d.). Multi-hazard emergency planning for schools site index. Retrieved from https://training.fema.gov/programs/emischool/el361toolkit/siteindex.htm#item10.

Georgia Department of Education. (2018). School safety assessment. Retrieved from www.gadoe.org/Curriculum-Instruction-and-Assessment/Curriculum-and-Instruction/Documents/School%20Safety%20Assessment.pdf.

Jennings, W. G., Khey, D. N., Maskaly, J., & Donner, C. M. (2011). Evaluating the relationship between law enforcement and school security measures and violent crime in schools. *Journal of Police Crisis Negotiations, 11*(2), 109–124. doi:10.10 80/15332586.2011.581511

Kleck, G. (2009). Mass shootings in schools: The worst possible case for gun control. *American Behavioral Scientist, 52*(10), 1447–1464. doi:10.1177/0002764209332557

Krehnke, M. (2015). Crime prevention through environmental design. *Information Systems Security*. Retrieved from www.infosectoday.com/Articles/CPTED.htm.

Lambert, R. D., & McGinty, D. (2002). Law enforcement officers in schools: Setting priorities. *Journal of Educational Administration, 40*(2), 257–273. Retrieved from https://saintleo.idm.oclc.org/login?url=https://search-proquest-com.saintleo.idm. oclc.org/docview/220444544?accountid=4870.

Rooney, T. (2015). Higher stakes—the hidden risks of school security fences for children's learning environments. *Environmental Education Research, 21*(6), 885–898. doi:10.1080/13504622.2014.936308

Stanley, M. S. (1996). School uniforms and safety. *Education and Urban Society, 28*(4), 424–435. Retrieved from http://web.b.ebscohost.com/ehost/pdfviewer/ pdfviewer?vid=1&sid=20931cfd-8507-4870-b76c-526b15c07abc%40session mgr103.

Statista. (n.d.). Crime and law enforcement—active shooter incidents in the U.S. 2000–2017. Retrieved from www.statista.com/statistics/324995/ active-shooter-incidents-in-the-us.

Texas State University. (2018). Advanced law enforcement rapid response training. Retrieved from https://alerrt.org/page/about.

U.S. Department of Justice. (2013). *A study of active shooter incidents in the United States between 2000 and 2013*. Washington, DC.

U.S. Department of Justice. (2018). Active shooter resources. Retrieved from www. fbi.gov/about/partnerships/office-of-partner-engagement/active-shooter-resources.

Vasilogambors, M. (2018). Hundreds of new state gun laws: Most expand access. Retrieved from www.pewtrusts.org/en/research-and-analysis/blogs/ stateline/2018/03/02/hundreds-of-new-state-gun-laws-most-expand-access.

Wade, K., & Stafford, M. (2003). Public school uniforms: Effect on perceptions of gang presence, school climate, and student self-perceptions. *Sage Journals*. Retrieved from http://journals.sagepub.com/doi/abs/10.1177/0013124503255002# articleCitationDownloadContainer.

Chapter 3

Addressing School Violence through Interdisciplinary Systems Change

Susan Kinsella and Nancy Wood

The recent occurrences of school violence have created a national crisis that requires a response by our communities to engage in a national dialogue with school administrators, teachers, parents, students, local resources, legislators, criminal justice professionals, and residents of the community. Violence in schools has become an epidemic and emergency responses are needed immediately if children and parents are to feel safe in a learning environment on a daily basis. Mental health practitioners who understand trauma have called for a system change that requires a comprehensive look at students, the school environment, resources, and community partnerships.

What proactive and positive approaches can administrators take to be prepared for this systems change? This chapter will present the idea of developing an interdisciplinary approach that includes administration, faculty, parents, students, and community partners. This is a step in the right direction, but it requires a new collaborative approach with educators, administrators, social workers, health and mental health professionals, criminal justice officials, legislators, religious leaders, and our business community.

It is essential to create school-community partnerships (with service, civic, religious, business, and others) that would assist with coordination of resources (such as violence-intervention training for teachers, creation of a violence-prevention program for high-risk students, access to referral of community mental health services, continued funding for these resources, and ongoing evaluation of these services) and bring together an interdisciplinary school crisis team to review the crisis response plan on an ongoing basis and determine where gaps exist and decide how to address them.

ADMINISTRATIVE SYSTEMS CHANGE

The recent and increased incidents of school violence require an immediate response by our communities to engage in a national dialogue concerning the necessity of administrative systems changes. A review of the literature indicates it is necessary to bring a balanced approach to school safety by a mix of interdisciplinary practices. These include the:

- creation of school-community partnerships to enhance school safety measures;
- development of crisis plans;
- implementation of preparedness training;
- review of communication systems within the school district and with community responders;
- inclusion of violence-prevention programs;
- introduction of peaceful conflict resolution and positive interpersonal relationship skills curricula to students; and
- use of evidence-based practices (Cowan & Paine, 2015).

With school violence being at the forefront of today's news, schools across the nation are confronted daily on how to keep students safe from gun violence. However, the conversation needs to go beyond the gun debate, and focus on identifying administrative strategies to improve overall safety. It is time to rely on research and evidence-based practices to give us some guidance in this area. In February 2018, an interdisciplinary group of 2,300 nationwide experts created a call for action that offers direction on policy and a list of recommendations (Interdisciplinary Group on Preventing School and Community Violence, 2018).

This call to action involves three levels of prevention, which include "universal approaches in promoting safety and well-being for everyone; practices for reducing risk and promoting protective factors for persons experiencing difficulties; and interventions for individuals where violence is present or appears imminent" (Interdisciplinary Group on Preventing School and Community Violence, 2018, para. 3). This direction on school safety policy and gun violence prevention can lay the groundwork for the conversation on creating a school-community partnership team, improve communication systems, support active shooter incident training, and provide mental health programs (www.nasponline.org).

This type of administrative systems change needs to happen swiftly and consistently across all school districts in the United States with a foundation of these best practices laying the framework for a safer school experience for our children. It will require coordinated efforts by districts in determining the costs for these necessary programs and the identification of funding sources and partnerships with our business communities to build this safety net.

Schools play an integral role in keeping students safe. As outlined in the *Call for Action to Prevent Gun Violence in the United States of America*, numerous education and mental health groups and various leading experts provide a framework for schools to follow a public health approach to address school shootings. The call to action outlines a research-based approach to violence prevention and response that addresses social and emotional health. To create a climate of safety, school systems should focus on prevention measures that increase access to mental health services and initiate programs for reducing risk factors toward violence.

The National Conflict Resolution Center (NCRC) is a recognized international leader in providing resources and training to communities in managing and solving conflicts (National Conflict Resolution Center, n.d.). Restorative circles are used in the NCRC's restorative justice work. This conflict-management strategy may be helpful in teaching respect and tolerance in school settings. The need to include conflict-resolution and interpersonal skills in our education curricula is evident in helping students to interact positively with their classmates, teachers, and administrators. Much has been written about the detrimental use of social media by children and adolescents who have not developed adequate methods of face to face communication. In a recent study by the Harvard Graduate School of Education, researchers found a significant increase in depression and suicidal thoughts for teens over the past several years, especially girls and those who spend multiple hours a day using screens (Shafer, 2017).

The classroom can be a safe place for children and adolescents to learn how to communicate positively and effectively with others on a face-to-face basis. Understanding the consequences of negative and destructive remarks made on social media should be part of a school curricula on building effective interpersonal relationships.

INTERDISCIPLINARY PROACTIVE AND POSITIVE APPROACHES

As school administrators continue to work on preventing school violence, there are proactive approaches that administrators can take to achieve a safe learning environment. An important step for any school administrator is to bring together an interdisciplinary school crisis team to review the school's crisis response plan and determine where the gaps are and how to address those gaps. Schools can benefit from the expertise and support of community organizations with the help of parents and students, who want to feel empowered and should be involved in the process. Other individuals to be part of this team, in addition to teachers, should be a school nurse, a school mental health professional, and security personnel.

School crisis team efforts should include creation of school-community partnerships with law enforcement agencies, emergency responders, local public health entities, and other relevant community members to identify concerns and assist with the coordination of various resources. These resources would include:

- violence intervention training for teachers;
- violence prevention programs for high-risk children and teens;
- securing funding for services from business communities;
- creating mentorships for students with community agencies; and
- establishing access to mental health services for students and teachers.

Once the team is formulated, the next step is for roles and procedures to be defined, with the underlying goal of a shared commitment to safeguard the well-being and safety of all members in a school community.

Depending on the size of the school district in the county, a school district may have two or more interdisciplinary crisis teams to support crisis preparation and handle response efforts. Under the leadership of the principal and student services team, a school-based crisis team is interdisciplinary and collaborates with community-based organizations to provide education and information on mental health services and support a continuum of care for teachers, staff, parents, and students (Schonfeld & Newgass, 2003).

Often comprised of school counselors, local law enforcement, fire department personnel, social workers, school nurses, pediatricians, and school psychologists, a district-based crisis team provides direct support and consultation to school staff, students, and families (Schonfeld & Newgass, 2003). Besides providing support after a traumatic event, the district-based intervention team delivers crisis training that covers the fundamentals in crisis preparation and response strategies for teachers, staff, and administrators.

A possible third team would be a regional resource team that would include some of the district-level members and community professionals from the human services community. The role of the resource group would be providing a forum for the sharing of experiences between districts, determining the resource needs for the region, advocating for additional state or federal services, and facilitating resources between districts (Schonfeld & Newgass, 2003).

Past experiences have shown that having a regional resource team can lead to a district-level organizational model and policies, the beginning of school staff trainings, and the expansion of mental health services through advocacy (Schonfeld & Newgass, 2003). It is important to recognize the services students need before, during, and after a school crisis. Resources should be offered in all languages needed for students and their families, including print, audio, and visual materials (www.nasponline.org).

Regarding interdisciplinary efforts in schools, on January 23, 2018, the National Association of School Psychologists (NASP) adopted a resolution supporting efforts to prevent gun violence (NASP, 2018). This resolution guides the NASP's important work and outlines their advocacy concerning public policies and school safety practices (NASP, 2018). The NASP works tirelessly to address gun violence that affects children through research-based efforts that lead to the advancement of effectual practices to improve students' behavior and mental health.

The National Association of School Resources Officers (NASRO) is a leader in school-based policing and trains school police officers. Regarding arming teachers, NASRO strongly recommends that only trained school resource officers (SROs) be allowed to carry firearms (Rock, 2018).

NASRO provides various reasons as to why they oppose arming a teacher or non-uniformed staff member and suggests that more funding would be best served to place SROs in every school (Rock, 2018). In 2017, the NASP and the NASRO published an updated best practices consideration for schools to "determine to what extent they need armed assailant training and to conduct trainings that make best use of resources, maximize effectiveness and minimize physical and psychological risks" (NASP & NASRO, 2017, p. 2).

An area that should be considered is the expansion or development of a reserve or part-time law enforcement program within the school system. Involving criminal justice professionals as community partners is another way to enhance our administrative systems change efforts. Many retired officers could either work part-time or volunteer their time to continue their service to the public. These law enforcement officers could supplement the SRO programs and would add another layer of protection to our educational institutions.

A key strategy in addressing solutions to lessen the fear of school safety in the minds of administrators, teachers, staff, parents, and students is by educating the school community through communication and training. By creating a culture of awareness, the community can effectively manage the day-to-day safety concerns, as well as handle a crisis that could happen at a moment's notice. By providing press releases, the community would be aware of the school district's efforts in addressing school safety and crisis preparedness (NASP School Safety and Crisis Response Committee, 2015). Through training, school personnel would immediately know how to react when a crisis occurs.

This important information should be readily available on a school's website and continuously updated with new information. There are crisis communication and management organizations that will provide active shooter training to educate schools to establish a culture of security and safety. For example, ALICE (alert, lockdown, inform, counter, evacuate) training offers a framework as follows:

- establish a proactive rather than passive policy;
- ensure the policy aligns with federal guidelines; and
- mandate teacher and student training on a scheduled basis (Active Shooter Response Training, n.d.).

ASSESSING SCHOOL SAFETY

Once teams are established, a formal review is conducted of the school safety policies and procedures to determine the school's crisis plans and emergency response procedures (NASP School Safety and Crisis Response Committee, 2015). When a school assesses their current practices and policies in school safety, administrators should ensure that the school facilities are equipped with the necessary support and systems to protect students, staff, and teachers from danger.

The National Association of School Psychologists has developed the *Framework for Safe and Successful Schools*, which offers a tool in assessing the current practices and policies of a school and helps in identifying solid systems that require continuous efforts, as well as important components that necessitate change to improve support for the school and student safety (Cowan, Vaillancourt, Rossen, & Pollitt, 2013). This book can be found on their website (www.nasponline.org) and includes three areas: policy recommendations, assessing the safety of the school environment, and action steps for implementing the framework. Tools and forms are provided for use by the schools.

Trauma is also a serious problem associated with school violence. When children feel threatened it can have a lasting psychological, emotional, or behavioral impact. Nearly 35 million children have experienced at least one event that could lead to childhood trauma (Child and Adolescent, 2012). So having the appropriate resources to deal with the aftermath of violence in our schools can affect the ability of our children to learn. Therefore, the addition of an accurate assessment system is essential.

It is also important to consider the profile of school violence perpetrators. In the last several years, young adult males have been primarily responsible for the shootings on school campuses. In the days following the attacks the media have presented a picture of these youths as emotionally disturbed, possible victims of bullying, often with underlying family dysfunction as well as school difficulties and academic failures. A thorough assessment of high-risk students is also needed to determine if resources are available as a prevention measure.

In the *Adverse Childhood Experience Study* (Felitti, 2003), researchers found that in a sample of 26,000 adults, many had experienced adverse childhood experiences that were common, concealed, and often unrecognized. Children are often adept at hiding issues due to shame, social taboos, and other consequences. Psychosocial experiences such as physical abuse, emotional abuse, and sexual abuse; growing up in a household with an alcoholic or drug user; a lack of a parent or guardian; growing up in a violent household; having an imprisoned family member or a mentally ill, chronically depressed, or institutionalized family member; one's mother being treated violently; and having both biological parents not present are correlated with organic disease, social malfunctions, and mental illness.

Adverse childhood experiences (ACES) produce neurodevelopmental and emotional damage, and impair social and school performance. It was found that ACES still have a profound effect fifty years later, although now transformed from a psychosocial experience into organic disease, social malfunction, and mental illness, and shaping adult life. Adverse childhood experiences are the main determinant of the health and social well-being of the nation.

ACES are widespread and typically go unrecognized. By adolescence, children have sufficient skill and often seek refuge from the trauma through use of alcohol, sexual promiscuity, smoking tobacco, using psychoactive materials, and overeating. If we are to assume that teens involved in school shootings have been identified as having one or more of the ACES characteristics, then it becomes essential to prevent further school tragedies by routinely screening at the earliest possible point for adverse childhood experiences. Primary prevention is possible and the literature suggests doing numerous screenings for ACES through common medical evaluations.

The solution requires a multi-pronged approach with a national awareness of ACES and mental health issues, identification of high-risk students, use of a valid assessment tool, development of a treatment plan for the student and their family, more resources for the student and family members, referrals to community agencies and local mental health services, the addition of more mental health services, development of peer support services in the schools, and bullying prevention programs (Ko et al., 2008).

The Aces Connection is a website that provides a trauma informed toolkit with information and resources on how to identify ACES, do assessments, and link community agencies. It explains how officials of local agencies can form coalitions between child welfare, animal welfare, domestic violence response teams, and adult protective services to identify cases of animal abuse and interpersonal violence. The website gives examples of how collaboration can be used to identify those children who may be suffering due to one or more adverse childhood experiences.

ACES profoundly shape a child's life and behavior, with remaining issues as they age, so early assessment and intervention are optimal. "Childhood experiences, both positive and negative, have a tremendous impact on future violence victimization and perpetration, and lifelong health and opportunity" (CDC, n.d., para. 1). Bullying is considered an adverse childhood experience and may lead to negative mental health effects and physical health consequences, as presented in a comprehensive review of bullying research in the National Academies of Sciences, Engineering and Medicine's report (Preventing Bullying through Science, Policy, and Practice, 2016).

This report suggests addressing ACES at an early age through preventive practices (Preventing Bullying through Science, Policy, and Practice, 2016). Some strategies include trauma-informed teams; building social-emotional skills; teaching mindfulness; implementing circle discussions, and practicing restorative justice (Preventing Bullying through Science, Policy, and Practice, 2016).

Research shows that victims of bullying are more likely to carry a weapon (gun, knife, or club) for fear of safety (Pham, Schapiro, John, & Adesman, 2017). In 2015, forty-five school shootings occurred with researchers wanting to investigate why students felt compelled to bring a gun to school (Pham et al., 2017). Data was analyzed from the national 2015 Youth Risk Behavior survey from grades 9 to 12 with 15,624 responses (Pham et al., 2017). Findings revealed one in five (20 percent) students reported being bullied in the previous year; broken down by gender, 16 percent were boys and 25 percent were girls, with 4.1 percent of students reported bringing a weapon to school (Pham et al., 2017). "The alarming percentage of students who carry weapons on school property signals that school campuses are still not the optimal, safe learning environments that we want for our youth" (Pham et al., 2017, p. 6).

Researchers Holt and Gini (2017) further add the importance of studying other risks and protective factors related to bullying and weapon carrying, such as suicidal ideation, substance abuse, resiliency, and a strong social network. Holt and Gini (2017) state, "Some recognized protective social factors for youth who have experienced bullying victimization include, for example, parental and peer support, positive relationships with teachers, attachment to the school, and sense of belonging" (p. 2). Further, they recommend parents, school personnel, and pediatricians should be watchful for signs of bullying and to start a dialogue with the youth to address their safety concerns (Holt &

Gini, 2017). Bullying prevention instructs students on the principle of respect and how to respond to the bullying of others, as well as providing teachers and staff with response strategies (Ross, Horner, & Stiller, n.d.).

More school districts are rethinking their zero-tolerance policies and implementing restorative justice practices (RJP) and bullying prevention (BP) strategies that encourage productive student behavior (Swain-Bradway & Sisaye, 2016). "Restorative practices is an emerging social science that studies how to strengthen relationships between individuals as well as social connections within communities" (International Institute for Restorative Practices, n.d., para. 2). With the use of restorative language, restorative justice practices are responsive strategies to address conflict, build relationships, and create a sense of community (Swain-Bradway & Sisaye, 2016). The RJP and BP guidelines are both aligned with the empirical-based framework of School-Wide Positive Behavior Interventions and Supports (SWPBIS) (Swain-Bradway & Sisaye, 2016).

The SWPBIS emphasizes strategies for teaching and supporting appropriate student behaviors for a positive school environment. The National Conflict Resolution Center is a recognized international leader in providing resources and training to communities in managing and solving conflicts (National Conflict Resolution Center, n.d.).

School districts need to review their policies and procedures and develop a framework for administrative change. Collaboration of schools, community partnerships, students, and parents is necessary for any real change to take place. Regional districts should work together to obtain necessary funding for essential services like mental health, emergency services, increased school resource officers, and health care in the schools.

New policies on the state and federal level can best be advocated for when coalitions of schools and community partners work together for change. Best practices should apply regarding the types of school assessments done and the services needed. Since adverse childhood experiences create trauma, which produces neurodevelopmental and emotional damage and impairs social and school performance, high-risk students for ACES should be assessed and treated quickly. Primary prevention should include the identification of all high-risk students.

We need to identify potential perpetrators in our school system and reach out to high-risk youth who may have underlying trauma due to an adverse childhood experience before any maladaptive behavior begins. The results of trauma do not go away. We need to recognize, screen, access, and treat ACES effectively in our schools, homes, and communities if we are to see a reduction in violent behavior demonstrated by our children and young adults.

REFERENCES

Active Shooter Response Training. (n.d.). *ALICE training program*. Retrieved from www.alicetraining.com.

Centers for Disease Control and Prevention (CDC). (n.d.). Adverse childhood experiences (ACEs). Retrieved from www.cdc.gov/violenceprevention/acestudy.

Cowan, K., & Paine, C. (2015). School safety: What really works. *Principal Leadership, 13*(7), 12. Retrieved from www.nasponline.org/resources/principals/March_13_School_Safety.

Cowan, K. C., Vaillancourt, K., Rossen, E., & Pollitt, K. (2013). *A framework for safe and successful schools* [Brief]. Bethesda, MD: National Association of School Psychologists. Retrieved from file:///C:/Users/drnan/AppData/Local/Packages/Microsoft.MicrosoftEdge_8wekyb3d8bbwe/TempState/Downloads/Framework_for_Safe_and_Successful_School_Environments%20(1).pdf.

Holt, M., & Gini, G. (2017, December). Complexities in the association between bullying victimization and weapon carrying. *American Academy of Pediatrics, 140*(6).

Interdisciplinary Group on Preventing School and Community Violence. (2018, February). *Call for action to prevent gun violence in the United States of America*. Retrieved from https://curry.virginia.edu/prevent-gun-violence.

International Institute for Restorative Practices (IIRP). (n.d.). What is restorative practices? Retrieved from www.iirp.edu.

Ko, S. J., Ford, J. D., Kassam-Adams, N., Berkowitz, S. J., Wilson, C., Wong, M., & Layne, C. M. (2008). Creating trauma-informed systems: Child welfare, education, first responders, health care, and juvenile justice. *Professional Psychology: Research and Practice, 39*(4), 396–404. Retrieved from http://dx.doi.org/10.1037/0735-7028.39.4.396.

NASP & NASRO. (2017). *Best practice considerations for schools in active shooter and other armed assailant drills* [Brief]. Bethesda, MD: National Association of School Psychologists. Retrieved from www.nasponline.org/armed-assailant-drills.

NASP School Safety and Crisis Response Committee. (2015). *Responding to school violence prevention: Guidelines for school administrators and crisis teams*. Bethesda, MD: National Association of School Psychologists. Retrieved from https://www.nasponline.org/resources-and-publications/resources/school-safety-and-crisis/school-violence-prevention/responding-to-school-violence-tips-for-administrators.

National Association of School Psychologists (NASP). (2018). Resolution supporting efforts to prevent gun violence. Retrieved from www.nasponline.org.

National Conflict Resolution Center. (n.d.). *About NCRC*. Retrieved from www.ncrconline.com.

Pham, T., Schapiro, L., John, M., & Adesman, A. (2017, December). Weapon carrying among victims of bullying. *American Academy of Pediatrics, 140*(6).

Preventing Bullying through Science, Policy, and Practice. (2016). F. Rivara and S. Le Menestrel, eds. *Committee on the biological and psychosocial effects of peer victimization: Lessons for bullying prevention*. Washington, DC: The National Academies Press. Retrieved from www.nap.edu/read/23482/chapter/1.

Rock, A. (2018, February 23). *ASRO recommends no firearms be on school campuses except for those carried by trained school resource officers.* Retrieved from www. campussafetymagazine.com/safety/nasro-opposes-arming-teachers.

Ross, S., Horner, R., & Stiller, B. (n.d.). Bully prevention in positive behavior support. Retrieved from www.stopbullying.gov/sites/default/files/2017-10/bullyprevention_ES.pdf.

Schonfeld, D. J., & Newgass, S. (2003, September). *School crisis response initiative.* Retrieved from https://ovc.gov/publications/bulletins/schoolcrisis/welcome.html.

Shafer, L. (2017, December 15). Social media and teen anxiety. *Harvard Graduate School of Education.* Retrieved October 28, 2017, from www.gse.harvard.edu/news/uk/17/12/social-media-and-teen-anxiety.

Simckes, M. (2017, July). Guns in America: The worrying relationship between school bullying and gun violence. *The Conversation.* Retrieved from https://theconversation.com/a-dangerous-mix-bullied-youth-report-access-to-loaded-guns-more-than-other-youth-79619.

Swain-Bradway, J., & Sisaye, S. (2016, March). *Restorative justice practices and bullying prevention.* Retrieved from www.stopbullying.gov/blog/2016/03/02/restorative-justice-practices-and-bullying-prevention.html.

RESOURCES

Schoolwide Positive Behavior Support: www.pbis.org/school

Understanding Bullying—Fact Sheet: www.cdc.gov/violenceprevention/pdf/Bullying_Factsheet.pdf

Chapter 4

A Practitioner's View of School Safety

A Walk in My Shoes

Jodi Lamb, Toni Zetzsche, and Fern Aefsky

This chapter reviews issues of school safety from the perspective of practitioners in schools. The organization of schools, school district and building leaders, and rules that impact the governance of schools must be part of ongoing conversations. School superintendents must work with their school boards and school attorneys when implementing change and managing needs around issues of school safety.

School boards in all districts in the United States are charged with the responsibility of developing and approving policies that govern all aspects of school operations. The school superintendent works with the school district personnel to implement those policies. School board attorneys work for the board, but work with the superintendent and other school leaders. They advise the board on issues, and issues of school safety are prevalent as a result of mass shootings that have occurred.

The National Association of School Boards has assembled resources for members, which can be found at www.nsba.org/services/school-board-leadership-services/school-safety-and-security. Their position statement includes the fact that all schools must be safe learning environments for all, and the resources they suggest are guidance to school boards in dealing with proactive, active, and reactive elements of school tragedies. While this is a good source of information, each school superintendent must work diligently with their own school board and school community in developing school safety plans.

Ensuring that these plans do not become "shelf art" is the responsibility of the school superintendent and other school leaders. In order for a policy to be successfully implemented across schools and district, the school administrators must ensure that the document's components are part of an integrated communication with stakeholders.

As stated in chapter 1, statistically, responses to school shootings are significant for three months after an event; then focus returns to pre-event status. The priorities change, and schools are institutions of learning, and focus is and should be on student learning outcomes. However, while school shootings, thankfully, do not occur often, the conversations and plans to protect our children must be part of an ongoing plan.

School superintendents and other central office administrators typically meet with police authorities to develop first response plans, and then other school leaders become part of the implementation team. School crisis team members then become part of the school-based planning team.

Building-level administrators need to be part of the initial conversations and solicited for input. Understanding that each building is different, the specificity of information school leaders can share should be surveyed and integrated into the district-level community conversations.

There are differences in states of how schools are organized. For example, Florida has sixty-seven school districts, as they are countywide districts. New York has over 690 school districts, as they are not countywide. These variances impact the issues around school safety.

SCHOOL ADMINISTRATORS' PERSPECTIVE

In the days following recent school tragedies, school principals find more of a multifaced approach to schoolwide safety is necessary to address growing concerns. A school principal's wide breadth of knowledge coupled with the broad level of responsibilities have often placed safety and security of the campus in the hands of district staff and school resource officers. Emergency management and crisis preparedness fell mid-level on the list of priorities for a building principal when identifying and prioritizing daily responsibilities.

More recently, due to violent attacks on schools, the role of managing school safety has become increasingly important, making it front and center on the list of priorities principals must address. In recent conversations across the nation on social media, it is easy to see the tide changing quickly and a strong focus on school safety taking over, with parents, students, policymakers, and educators looking to principals for change in school safety practices. Principals have felt greater pressure to evaluate their roles in crisis management. What was once a duty focused on fire and weather drills, now places greater emphasis on lockdowns and crisis planning.

Each morning principals across the nation spend at least a few minutes scanning the campus, thinking about locked gates, easily accessible doors, the perimeter of the campus, and possible issues with congestion, traffic, and their ability to keep students safe. This new focus often causes reason for pause as principals are not regularly trained to assess safety and security. Principals are instructional leaders and are not trained to identify possible breech points and emergency management protocols, though times are changing and so must the role of the building leader.

NEW PROCEDURES AND A CHANGING
CLIMATE FOR PRINCIPALS

In the wake of new security measures, greater emphasis on safety, and a movement to increase law enforcement presence on campus, school principals are taxed with participating in broad-scale activities that require participating in safety forums, training, and new programs addressing violence on campus. Campus lockdown procedures that required students and staff members to lockdown into a room and remain silent have been replaced by active shooter response plans with a more tactical approach. A 2016 report from the Government Accountability Office found that forty states, including Florida, require individual schools to perform exercises or drills to test their emergency plans with little to no federal coordination. Many school districts are adopting options-based approaches such as "run, hide, fight" to allow staff and students to practice and conduct drills using scenarios that require participants to make decisions based on the attacker or situation (Zdziarski, 2016).

As principals gain their footing in the new arena, the climate surrounding school safety is moving at a rapid pace. Changes are occurring before principals and civilian personnel can become familiar with new programs, policies, and state requirements. According to the U.S. Bureau of Labor Statistics, approximately 5 percent of all businesses experience an instance of workplace violence. For larger organizations with over one thousand employees, this rate is increased tenfold to 50 percent. Active shooter incidents reported by the FBI in a report titled *Active Shooter Incidents in the United States 2016 and 2017* designated fifty shootings across the nation as active shooter incidents (twenty in 2016 and thirty in 2017) (Federal Bureau of Investigation, 2018).

This report does not encompass all gun-related incidents, violence, or threats of violence on school campus as it focuses only on incidents designated as "active shooter." Though this information is limited in scope, it provides enough information to cause mass concern among parents and students and calls into question the preparedness of our campuses.

BUILDING A COLLABORATIVE PARTNERSHIP

Pasco County Schools (Florida) and the Pasco County Sheriff's Office provide a strong example of school and law enforcement collaboration as they have worked to create a unique partnership that encourages training, conversation and collaboration. Through this partnership an evaluation of campus safety and lockdown procedures led to the development of an Active Threat Plan. An adaptation of run, hide, fight calls for staff and students to practice making decisions based on the attacker, the location of the attacker, and their ability to escape or avoid the situation.

A strong partnership and continued conversations create a sense of security on campus and in the community as parents and students see and feel the increased presence during regular school days, during training exercises, and when low level threats occur. Utilizing the partnership allows for increased opportunity to talk with students, maintains a presence on campus, and provides deputies time to learn and understand the flow of the campus.

These partnerships are similar to those in most other districts across the United States. School leaders and local police authorities work together and have done so with rigor since the Columbine shooting in 1999. Each subsequent school shooting has resulted in a review of plans, legislation, and conversation among organizations and schools.

Through continued conversation, consistent assessment of practices, and well-trained school resource officers, police presence in schools has provided training opportunities for students, staff, and law enforcement officers across campuses. Utilizing school campuses and ensuring continued collaboration has created a greater sense of preparedness community wide.

Engaging stakeholders in conversations regarding school safety is becoming common practice in school districts today to provide parents and students a voice in creating a safe environment. Understanding safety concerns unique to each campus is essential as each campus setting provides varying dynamics, unique neighborhoods, and physical attributes that must be individually addressed.

During a recent town hall meeting (2018) in a school district in Florida, several students and parents voiced concern regarding the safety and security of campuses, picking apart unlocked gates, classrooms with windows that are accessible from the perimeter, the need for armed guards, and the need to tighten front office procedures. In another district in New York, students and parents asked school authorities how they could possibly maintain safe schools on open campuses, and how older facilities could be changed to be safer.

These are issues with no simple resolution. All facilities cannot be altered without significant resources and time. Ensuring that parent, student, teacher, and all other concerns are acknowledged is important for school leaders.

Transparency in dealing with issues of school safety has never been more important. Even if quick solutions are not possible, ongoing conversations and improvements enable school leaders to visibly share their goals with the public domain. The public know it is an issue of continued review, which makes stakeholders feel that responsibility of safety for all is a priority for the district.

STUDENT PERSPECTIVES

Many students have begun to take a closer look at safety and security as they witness their peers across the nation take an active role in assessing and discussing school safety. Student voice is ever present in schools today at the secondary level and has become increasingly louder as young adults are more and more aware of the issues surrounding school safety. Many schools have utilized student council as a focus group to discuss issues surrounding safety. Students ask questions regarding the physical safety of their peers from a very narrow perspective as they have limited background in assessing and analyzing current practice.

This narrow perspective begs the question among principals, *What can we do to create a more informed student population so that we may work collaboratively to address concerns?* How can a principal plan for safety without student input? How can we ask students to share information regarding threats, possible threats, or concerns if we do not give them a voice at the table?

In Pasco County, Florida, the students were given a voice at the table during several roundtable discussions called the student congress. Each secondary school selected a small group of students to ask questions, take part in conversation, and act as the voice of the student body regarding safety concerns on campus. Students participating shared concerns, asked questions, and provided input that will be used at the school and district level to address safety on campus.

TEACHER PERSPECTIVES

It is almost impossible to enter a department meeting, a lounge, or the copy room without a conversation about recent events related to school safety occurring. Teachers are increasingly aware of their surroundings and by nature aware of the pulse of the school and student body. On the front lines, teachers have a stronger voice than ever in creating a safe environment. Each day new ideas and concerns are discussed and principals across the nation are making changes to plans, policies, action plans, and expectations based on teacher input.

Teachers know the campus, they know the students, and they know the "feeling" in the air on any given day. Teachers are more and more in tune with the daily interactions of their students and take every opportunity to know their students personally to ensure quick identification of needs, concerns, or issues.

While comments, questions, and concerns are essential in the true evaluation of current practice, much of the focus remains physical. Physical perimeter, layout, fencing, and check-in procedures are important but do not address tactics and response should violence occur. Peruzza et al. (2016) addressed the need for education and communication between stakeholders and school resource officers to engage parents and students in realistic conversations about school safety.

In conversations with staff, they have become even more vigilant in regards to locking doors and using opportunities for conversation to analyze the stability of those who seem "off" or agitated. Taking a more proactive approach to discussions surrounding low-level threats is something many staff members have commented on in recent times. Often stakeholders address school safety from an unrealistic perspective, calling attention to locks, windows, and barricades rather than focusing on practices that increase safety through supervision, monitoring, and engagement.

ADDRESSING MORE THAN PHYSICAL SAFETY

The obligation extends further beyond campus security in isolation and addresses physical, emotional, and academic safety. Historically, campus safety focused primary efforts on physical safety and the physical plant. Addressing stakeholders is cyclical, as the impact of each is essential to understand. In a study conducted by Bosworth, Ford, and Hernandaz (2011), physical safety and security features were overwhelmingly addressed.

School safety efforts often led to metal detectors, card systems, and fencing, addressing the issue from a physical plant perspective rather than looking at planning and preparation, drill procedures, and training of staff. Addressing safety from practices associated with monitoring often leads to a conversation related to mental health. Principals have called for greater emphasis on research-based and systemic solutions. The call for a multifaceted and interdisciplinary framework is clear.

Addressing the root cause, the foundation, calls for strengthened prevention and support programs. Bullying and harassment programs, violence-prevention programs, and increased access to mental health counseling are among the solutions presented by principals during every meeting and conversation focused on school safety.

In a study conducted by Bosworth, Ford, and Hernandaz (2011), mental health accessibility played a strong role in perceptions about the safety of a school and the measures by which students feel safe among peers. This calls attention to the need for greater accessibility and support on campus for students experiencing mental-health-related issues. To ensure schoolwide safety measures are utilized, principals must address faculty perceptions regarding school safety and create an environment where staff actions ease parent and student concerns.

As school leadership maintains a footing in planning and preparation, it has become commonplace for principals to build their own partnerships with programs and mental health providers to ensure needs are met. With little support available in most schools, much of the work to address the needs of students with mental health concerns falls to guidance counselors and social workers. Though the staff is willing, the work often requires more extensive support beyond capability and training. Creating opportunities to address mental-health-related issues is becoming essential and no longer a secondary priority.

PLANT OPERATIONS AND FACILITY MANAGEMENT CONSIDERATIONS

This section addresses facility aspects of school safety for both existing structures and new construction. As each aspect is examined, questions are posed to help administrators consider the advantages and disadvantages of each option. It is important to note that no one improvement or tool will prevent tragedy. A comprehensive safety program is critical. This part of the chapter looks closely at facility needs, but it should be considered as just one part of a comprehensive program.

Can the Facility Keep Us Safe?

When the shooter approached Sandy Hook Elementary, he encountered a locked front door that required a staff person to push a button to release the door. Not deterred, he shot his way in. Schools across the country have invested in ways to restrict access. Was it worth it? Restricting building entry makes it safer; it does not guarantee that nothing will go wrong.

Consider all of the safety measures banks have used for years. Do bank robberies still occur? Of course. Schools must still be welcoming and access-ible. No one wants a school to be a prison. Still, there are ways to increase the security of every campus.

Consider all of the different ways a building can be secure: fences around the perimeter, remote controlled locked entry doors with a buzzer system, security cameras, computer-controlled electronic locks, metal detectors, iden-tification of safe rooms, and bulletproof glass. Now consider the cost of these improvements. In the big scheme of things, the price tag for any or all of these items is insignificant if it saves lives. At the same time, a school or district budget can only be stretched so far.

Safety Features Added to Existing Structures

What exists in most schools? Doors with locks. However, how often is a classroom door unlocked when it should be locked? What procedures are in place to be sure that substitutes are provided appropriate keys and they are instructed to keep doors locked. How long does it take a teacher to find her keys and lock the door if she left it unlocked? Making sure that all doors have operating locks and ensuring that all staff have correct keys for their area and *use* them is a relatively insignificant cost.

Until the shooting at Marjory Stoneman Douglas High School in Parkland, Florida, no shooter had gone through a locked classroom door. Cruz, the shooter, broke the glass on a classroom door and shot into the classroom. As administrators know, the style of the classroom door varies from having no glass to having a large window, solid-core to hollow doors, and metal to wood. A change in door style with either no window or a small window may be an affordable improvement. Window tinting may serve to be far more affordable than replacement and several products are resistant to penetration. Installing solid doors with bulletproof glass is a vast improvement but may serve to be too costly for most districts.

Security cameras throughout a building certainly are a helpful tool for administrators in overall building safety. It is valuable when trying to deter-mine which student started a fight or who was the last one out of a bathroom before the detection of a fire in the trash can. Will it prevent the access of a shooter? No. Can it help to identify him after the fact? Yes. Can it be used to determine how well the staff and students followed established procedures during the event? Yes.

Do safe rooms exist in school? Schools in the Midwest are often designed with safe rooms to protect staff and students from tornados. However, in other parts of the country, inner rooms such as material closets, planning areas, or interior hallways that access restrooms may exist, but not for the purposes of a safe room. In an emergency, they can double as a safe room, if the students are trained to use it and if the staff has kept the area free from clutter. Could some rooms be repurposed so that overall renovation costs can be kept to a minimum while safety is increased?

Student Entry

How many ways can students enter a building? How many access points exist? Can access be limited? Can all traffic be forced through one entry point? Can multiple metal detectors be used or just one? Metal detectors can be a great addition to an overall safety program. However, procedurally there are some complicating factors.

Here are some to consider: How many ways do students enter the building? Budget for that many metal detectors *and* enough staff to operate them. While there is a huge range in the price for one walk-through metal detector, one that is affordable and reliable runs between $4,000 and $5,000. The cost of the detector is only the first investment.

A commitment to free up enough staff on a daily basis to man the detectors is a human capital cost that has to be addressed prior to a purchase. Plan on making six staff members available daily during arrival for each metal detector in use. Staff will have to supervise the students. They have to be kept two to three feet apart and have to be monitored to be sure they cannot hand something around the detection area.

Here are some other questions to consider regarding possible use of metal detectors: Are there ways that students can hand items over a fence to those who have already gone through detection? How long will the arrival process take? It will slow down considerably—especially if there is only one detector. Do students who ride the bus come in the same entrance as those who arrive by car? If not, you need another metal detector.

What happens with the late arrivals? Who will take them through the metal detector? Do late arrivals enter through the same entrance as those who came on buses? If not, you will need another metal detector. Are you only going to take students through it, or do all school visitors have to go through it too? If so, will the student metal detector be in the right location, or will you need another one?

If you consider that for each time you add another metal detector, it will cost on average $5,000 and tie up six people, monetarily it is a huge commitment. Regardless, it may serve as an important part of your overall security plan.

Will a fence keep my students safe? Limited access to campus can be achieved through the use of fences. There are many questions to consider: How big is your campus? Is it a 25 acre elementary or an 80 acre high school? Are the fences climbable? What about during arrival and dismissal? How can you control who has access while parents wait in the car rider line?

How much of the day does a section of the campus remain open? What time do parents start lining up for the car riders line? What time do the buses arrive? This is especially the case for schools that have more than one dismissal (i.e., pre-K dismissal before traditional elementary). Where do students go during fire drills and bomb threats? It is common knowledge that the shooter in Parkland pulled the fire alarm. Do they open the gates? Can the building stay secure while students and staff move far enough away to remain safe?

The topic of fences leads to another item. Some schools either have or will have embassy-like fences. These kind of fences are much stronger than chain-link fences. Depending on how they are constructed, they can be resistant to penetration by vehicles. Certainly, the idea of needing such a fence is completely foreign to most of us. But, did we really anticipate all of the school shootings that have occurred? If we are spending money to harden a facility, should we do so in preparation of a terrorist attack with explosives?

If your answer to that question is "yes," then penetration-resistant fences will be an investment to consider. The price of chain link is estimated to be about $20–$30 per foot depending on height and material. Typically, an elementary can be fenced for just under $200,000. Of course, for a concrete fence, that estimate should double.

Get a Safety Assessment Done before Making Any Decisions

If any or all of these safety measures are put in place, it certainly increases the level of safety provided. However, all of them require consistent operational policies and accountability for when they are not followed. Most safety experts take into account many more factors than just the condition of the facility. After all, any addition or innovation added to the facility is only as good as the people who use it. A safety expert can make recommendations to meet different budgets and community expectations.

Safety Features Incorporated into New Construction

What about safety features that can be added to new construction? As with the security measures for preexisting buildings, some measures are easily attainable and affordable and others are costly. Features, in addition to all of those above, that can be considered include penetration-resistant vestibules, limited entry points, and constructing buildings on higher ground with an "embassy-like" fence that is penetration resistant.

Vestibules can serve as an excellent option so that all human traffic filters through it. Many have been designed with systems that require visitors to scan their driver's license before access is granted. The scanned license is then reviewed by a web-based service like that offered by Raptor and cross-referenced to state and federal offender lists. If the license clears, a temporary badge is issued via a printer and access is granted.

Those vestibules can be designed to accommodate large numbers of students arriving with a sufficient number of metal detectors but, as stated previously, implementation will require a sufficient number of trained staff to keep the arrival process moving quickly and efficiently. Even without a vestibule described above, constructing an open design with limited access makes securing a building easier.

A campus with multiple buildings may be designed in a way that is aesthetically pleasing to the eye, but it is difficult to monitor student behavior and movement without an excessive number of staff available for supervision. While "nooks and crannies" give students a place to step away from the crowds, they also provide hiding places where unacceptable behavior can occur without notice. The addition of a significant number of cameras will assist in deterring a lot of inappropriate behavior, but keeping students moving is the best defense.

Experienced administrators can look quickly at a building and indicate how difficult it will be to supervise. When architects and administrators can work together on designs, supervision can get much easier.

Finally, where possible, district personnel are beginning to look at land parcels that can facilitate safety and security. If a school can be built up on a hill where the land has been cleared around it, it makes it easier for staff to monitor individuals approaching the building. While that certainly is not always an option, creating a clear path makes it easier to spot an oncoming threat. Some districts are exploring ways to include fences like one might see at an embassy. Cost is a huge factor since many high school campuses are built on 80 acres or more.

All of the items above focus on security measures that are enforced during the traditional school day. This does not address after-school and evening events. Think about a well-attended high school football game. How can these measures be implemented at such an event? Looking at airport security or large stadiums and the way that they are managed may help school officials develop procedures that can increase safety without minimizing access by the school community. Regardless, security at that level will incur a cost.

It is clear that there is no one solution that will solve the safety problems. The best solution is one that is multilayered with clear policies that are implemented with fidelity. The best security system is only as good as those involved in its use. As is stated by other authors, implementation requires a strong training program so that staff and students know what to do, know when to do so, and can do so habitually.

REFERENCES

Bosworth, K., Ford, L., & Hernandaz, D. (2011). School climate factors contributing to student and faculty perceptions of safety in select Arizona schools. *Journal of School Health, 81,* 194–201.

Federal Bureau of Investigation. (2018, April). Active shooter incidents in the United States in 2016 and 2017. Retrieved October 28, 2018, from www.fbi.gov/file-repository/active-shooter-incidents-us-2016-2017.pdf/view.

NEA. (2018). *NEA's School Crisis Guide.* Retrieved from http://healthyfutures.nea.org/wp-content/uploads/2015/05/schoolcrisisguide.pdf.

Passy, J. (2018). *Schools rethink building design to protect students from mass shooters.* Retrieved from www.marketwatch.com/story/how-schools-are-being-designed-to-protect-students-and-teachers-from-mass-shooters-2018-02-16.

Peruzza, L., Sarao, A., Barnaba, C., Bragato, P. L., Dusi, A., Grimaz, S., & Cravos, C. (2016). Teach and learn seismic safety at high school: The SISIFO project. *Bollettino Di Geofisica Teorica Ed Applicata, 57*(2), 129–146. doi:10.4430/bgta0157

Sandy Hook Advisory Commission. (2015). *Final report of the Sandy Hook commission.* State of Connecticut.

Winn, Z. (2018). *The pros and cons of installing metal detectors in schools.* Retrieved from www.campussafetymagazine.com/safety/metal-detectors-in-schools/.

Zdziarski II, E. L. (2016). Campus crisis: It's not just about responding. *Presidency, 19*(2), 26–30.

Chapter 5

Mental Health Considerations and Options for Schools

Courtney Wiest and Cindy Lee

A principal of a high school in New York shared his frustration that mental health support is critical for students, and not readily available. Proactive intervention is believed to be a missing component for school administrators to access.

In the Parkland shooting, the shooter had been identified with behavioral challenges since middle school. This student was transferred between schools six times in three years as a way of handling the problem. He was then transferred to a program for students with emotional educational disabilities, and then suspended from school for disciplinary reasons. He made threats against that school via email that was shared with teachers by school administrators. School system personnel requested an involuntary psychiatric evaluation as a result of school counselor and police (SRO) concerns, but the investigators from the state agency determined that he was not at risk for harming himself or others, and determined there was no basis for a psychiatric evaluation, even though he had posted disturbing, violent pictures of weapons on social media, had numerous racial, anti-Semitic posts, and posted statements of killing others, referencing intent to mimic a previous school shooting (Cox & Rich, 2018).

Many other school shootings have similar issues, of shooters being known to school personnel who have identified issues of concern and, then, a lack of sufficient resources to address those concerns. School leaders must have input and be a consistent part of all planning regarding school safety. While recognizing one plan will not meet the needs of all schools, a plan without significant consideration for addressing mental health concerns is less than helpful to students and schools.

The following sections of this chapter contain various options for schools and school stakeholders to consider regarding proactive, active, and reactive implementations of preventing acts of school violence.

PREVENTION AND INTERVENTION APPROACHES TO SCHOOL VIOLENCE THROUGH A TRAUMA-INFORMED CARE MODEL

Case Study

Jackson High school is located in Orange County, Florida. The overall school population is 2,800. There are an estimated 60 percent white students, 20 percent Hispanic students, 15 percent black students, and 5 percent other. The school has implemented a Positive Behavioral Interventions and Supports (PBIS) model, which identifies alternative behavior interventions to address the behavior concern instead of a punitive approach. Additionally, resources such as counseling, parental support, and academic remediation are provided to the students. The school was recognized by President Obama for this approach and the positive outcomes concerning reducing negative school behaviors. Additionally, the PBIS model has developed a culture of community and security at the school. The students feel empowered and motivated to keep the school safe.

In January 2017 a student viewed a threatening post on social media from one of her school peers. The post alluded to an act of school violence from the peer. As part of the PBIS implementation, the school set up a "see something say something" anonymous reporting system. The peer reported this concern to the reporting system and school authorities were able to inform the proper authorities. The school was fortunate; the authorities found weapons and an action plan to carry out a school shooting.

This case study highlights the prevention benefits with the implementation of a trauma-informed model. The school took multiple steps to develop, implement, and maintain a culture of community, security, and speaking out for the school as a whole. As you review the chapter, think how this could have ended differently without the implementation of this model.

Over the last decade school violence and safety has increased drastically. Children and school personnel are being impacted daily by threats of violence or acts of violence. Since January 2018 there have been over twenty active school shooting incidences. That is an average of one heartbreaking school shooting every week. These tragic events have shocked the world.

This has resulted in school communities being fractured and left to pick up the pieces. Additionally, the National Survey of Children Exposed to

Violence found that 60 percent of the children surveyed have been exposed to some form of trauma, either in or out of school (Treatment and Service Adaptive Center, n.d.). Furthermore, Burke et al. (2011) found in a study of 701 participants that children who are exposed to four or more traumas are thirty-two times more likely to be labeled as learning disabled (Wiest & Lee, 2016). One way school communities can work together to have a prevention and intervention model is to foster a supportive environment and implement a trauma-informed school model (Wiest & Lee, 2016).

With the drastic increase in societal mass killings, in particular, schools shootings and violent events, school communities, parents, and the nation as a whole seek to identify approaches to provide safety and security for children in the school setting. This chapter will discuss an overview of trauma on children within school systems; discuss the implication of a trauma-informed model for teachers, administrators, and parents; identify tools that can be utilized in schools; and provide resources needed for a trauma-informed school.

Definition of Trauma and PTSD Symptoms

Trauma events are defined as incidents that are perceived as terrifying, shocking, sudden, or that potentially pose a threat to one's life, safety, or personal integrity (Black, Woodsworth, Tremblay, & Carpenter, 2012; Wiest & Lee, 2016). Traumatic events can be natural disasters such as hurricanes or earthquakes, or they can be human-made disasters such as terrorism, domestic violence, and mass shootings. Traumatology research has shown most people respond to a wide range of traumatic events in similar ways. The common responses include traumatic responses, post-traumatic stress responses, and post-traumatic stress disorder (PTSD) (Black et al., 2012; Suarez et al., 2012; Wiest & Lee, 2016). The primary symptoms for PTSD as defined by the *DSM 5* are:

1) history of an identifiable traumatic event;
2) re-experiencing of the trauma;
3) avoidance of cues associated with the trauma or emotional numbing; and
4) symptoms of increased arousal.

If a person experiences these stressors for more than six months and they are disruptive to their normal functioning, then it is considered post-traumatic stress disorder (American Psychiatric Association, 2013). These symptoms can manifest as variations such as anger, depression, increased startle responses, and so on. Black et al. (2012) notes symptoms can often be misdiagnosed if one is not assessed through a trauma-informed lens (Wiest & Lee, 2016).

A key part of the definition of a traumatic event is the individual's perception of trauma. An individual may experience similar events; however, the individual's response and interpretation of the event will impact the level of trauma the individual experiences (Wiest & Lee, 2016). Black et al. (2012) discussed the importance of considering the individual's perception when planning for prevention and intervention services (Wiest & Lee, 2016).

Impact of Trauma on Children: Risk of Being Misdiagnosed/ Mislabeled

Current research highlights the impact of traumatic events in children. These events impact childhood development socially, emotionally, and cognitively. Research has found children exposed to trauma are at greater risk of being developmentally delayed and demonstrate inferior school readiness. Black et al. (2012), in their review of the literature, described the prevalence of trauma exposure and the impact of trauma on adolescents' physical and psychological development.

One out of every four adolescents has experienced at least one traumatic event (Wiest & Lee, 2016). Even with these startling statistics, there has been limited intervention focusing on trauma-informed care or treatment. Many times children experiencing traumatic stress are mislabeled and misdiagnosed with attention deficit disorder, oppositional-defiant disorder, and other diagnoses (Wiest & Lee, 2016).

In response to the rise of mass traumatic events and trauma by children and adults, the concept of trauma-informed care has emerged. This concept is defined by the Substance Abuse and Mental Health Services Administration (SAMHSA) (2013): when a human service program or school takes the step to become trauma-informed, every part of the organization, including management and service delivery systems, must be modified to include a basic understanding of how trauma affects the life of an individual seeking service (SAMHSA, 2013).

Six Principles for a Trauma-Informed Model or Organization

According to SAMHSA (2015), there are six key principles in developing a trauma-informed model or organization:

1. safety;
2. trustworthiness and transparency;
3. peer support;

4. collaboration and mutuality;
5. empowerment, voice, and choice; and
6. cultural, historical, and gender issues (SAMHSA, 2015).

A key factor in developing a trauma-informed model is that all school personnel are instrumental in the process. It cannot be the role of one department; it must be implemented downward from administration to all staff. All school personnel must be trained and know how to respond to individual students or mass school needs should a catastrophic event occur.

NEEDS AND IMPLICATIONS FOR STUDENTS

Students impacted by trauma face a variety of challenges and needs. According to the National Child Traumatic Stress Network (NCTSN) (2008; Wiest & Lee, 2016) one in four children are impacted by a traumatic event, which directly reflects on their ability to learn, and students present with behavioral symptoms. NCTSN outlined the following areas as potential signs of trauma for students in school:

1. school performance—lower GPA, attendance, higher dropout, increased suspensions/expulsions, and decrease in reading readiness;
2. increased responses in the classroom and at home—jumpiness, fidgety, sleep disturbance, moodiness, anger, and social withdrawal; and
3. emotional and physical distress—somatic complaints, poor emotional control, impulsive behavior, change in school performance, and hyperreactive to sounds (NCTSN, 2008; Wiest & Lee, 2016).

A Trauma-Informed Model for Schools

Implementing a trauma-informed model as prevention, intervention, or crisis response includes the following recommendation by NCTSN:

1. Maintain a sense of normalcy and routine.
2. Give students a sense of control by allowing choices when appropriate.
3. Have a designated support staff for children exposed to trauma.
4. Develop boundaries for appropriate behavior and incorporate a positive behavior model.
5. Provide time to have children process the trauma.
6. Clarify misconceptions about the trauma verbalized by students.

7. Be mindful of environmental factors that may trigger a stress response after the trauma.
8. Make sure students are not bombarded by questions and curiosity after the trauma.
9. Be aware of at-risk behaviors and refer students to identified services (NCTSN, 2008; Wiest & Lee, 2016).

Trauma-Informed Model for School Communities

School communities that can develop a trauma-informed model that incorporates these strategies can foster an environment that reduces the negative impact of trauma on students (NCTSN, 2008). In the case study, the school developed an anonymous reporting system. This empowers students to take control of their school and gain a sense of safety.

Furthermore, these strategies should be implemented after school-wide traumatic events to assist in the healing process. Over the last few years we have witnessed students becoming activists, attending legislation events, and staging walkouts to voice their concerns about school safety. These type of activities give the students a sense of control and empowerment after an event. It is essential for the school community to foster these type of activities while maintaining boundaries and safety at the school to continue the healing process.

IMPLICATIONS AND SUGGESTIONS FOR SCHOOL ADMINISTRATORS

School administrators are key in developing a Trauma-Informed School Model (TISM). Administrators must have an outline plan. This plan should include procedures, policies, and key roles in the process. Walkley and Cox (2013) stressed the importance for the school administration to foster a safe environment. This can assist in the prevention and intervention stages of an event. Administrators need to be aware of students impacted by trauma, then identify key staff to assist in security procedures, supportive counseling, as well as ongoing education for teachers and paraprofessional administration (NCTSN, 2008; Walkley & Cox, 2013; Wiest & Lee, 2016).

Another prevention and intervention approach many schools are utilizing across the United States is providing a safe and therapeutic classroom for students. These schools are doing this by implementing a Positive Behavioral Interventions and Supports model. This model is a school-wide approach to managing behavior by implementing positive-based intervention strategies. By rewarding and promoting positive behaviors, students develop a sense of community and integrity, holding each other accountable for their actions (McIntosh, Campbell, Carter, & Dickey, 2009; Wiest & Lee, 2016).

Implementing these approaches promotes a school culture of safety that calls for action when concerning behaviors develop. This also allows the students to have a sense of control and action over their environment.

Along with fostering a safe and secure environment, school administration is crucial in educating teachers and support staff regarding the growing needs of students impacted by trauma. Each administrator should develop and keep an ongoing education plan for teachers and staff that addresses the plan, resources, and needs of the students (NCTSN, 2008). Each school should have a comprehensive threat assessment, plan, and team. Lastly, transparent communication is vital in fostering a trauma-informed environment (Walkley & Cox, 2013; and Wiest & Lee, 2016).

IMPLICATIONS AND SUGGESTIONS FOR TEACHERS

Teachers have the highest level of interaction with students. Therefore, teachers have an essential role in prevention and intervention. Teachers are often the first to identify, support, and provide for the needs of the students. Along with a school-wide PBIS model, teachers should engage students in positive coping and relaxation skills daily. These skills should be embedded in the daily lessons. Some techniques are:

1. deep breathing;
2. positive imagery; and
3. taking a small timeout to regroup (Anderson, Christenson, Sinclair, & Lehr, 2004).

Introducing students to these techniques before an event can equip students with the proper tools to handle and manage the stress before and after a critical incident unfolds. These skills not only assist children in dealing with past stressors or trauma, but also give them positive skills to handle future stress (Stein et al., 2003; Wiest & Lee, 2016).

Trauma-Informed Model for Classroom Environment

The classroom environment is a key factor to examine in a trauma-informed model. Teachers should be educated and given adequate resources to provide a friendly, warm environment. The environment should be visually pleasing and provide a sense of security. Here are some guidelines from the Center for Teacher Effectiveness (n.d.) to provide a safe, secure environment:

1. desk arrangement;
2. color selection;
3. light;
4. music; and
5. scent (Center for Teacher Effectiveness, n.d.; Wiest & Lee, 2016).

Creating a Sense of Community in the Classroom

Students should feel connected to each other, the teacher, and the school. The classroom should promote social learning, safety, and security. By doing this, the students have a culture of protecting each other. Students know each other and can speak out when there are concerns with their peers. The case study illustrated the sense of community and concern a peer had for a friend who posted a concerning post on social media. This sense of community and connection fostered a sense to speak out and take action.

Strategies for Promoting a Trauma-Informed Model for Classroom Environment

Additionally, this provides a network of support when faced with challenges and stressors to help alleviate feelings and symptoms associated with PTSD (Anderson et al., 2004). Some ways teachers can promote this environment include:

1. weekly classroom meetings;
2. planning walls;
3. concern corners; and
4. problem solution groups.

These opportunities allow students to join together and have ownership over the classroom. They also foster a sense of community for each other. Lastly, after an event, this type of opportunity can be an avenue for change and advocating, which aids the healing process.

IMPLICATIONS FOR PARENTS

Parent involvement and engagement are critical in developing a trauma-informed model. Parents can support school personnel and provide vital information. Schools should engage parents early on in the process of prevention and intervention. Schools can do this by providing informational sessions, school events to foster community, and regular opportunities for parents to provide feedback (Anderson et al., 2004).

Parents should be encouraged to communicate with administrators when concerns arise at home. This open communication allows for support staff to intervene and provide services. Early intervention can reduce the number and level of critical events (Anderson et al., 2004).

Relevant Resources for a Trauma-Informed Model

There are several online resources to educate and inform school personnel and parents regarding the benefits, challenges, and needs of children impacted by trauma. The resources are outlined below with a summary of the information at the site:

- Treatment and Service Adaptive Center website (https://traumaaware schools.org). This online resource provides an in-depth review of childhood trauma and multiple resources for schools, administrators, teachers, parents, and the general public. The site also offers several short video clips from experts on an array of topics related to trauma in children. Lastly, the site has many "how to" guides for school planning and implementation purposes.
- Time to Teach (www.timetoteachtrainer.com). This site provides over forty years of knowledge, research, and experience in setting a classroom environment. The website provides teachers with evidenced-based research on how to develop a classroom that fosters a sense of connection and community. The website also gives basic tips from desk arrangements to a structured classroom positive behavior model.
- Positive Behavioral Intervention and Supports (PBIS) (www.pbis.org). The site offers resources for schools, parents and families, and the community. The site also provides evaluation feedback, resources, and reports on the PBIS model. Lastly, the site provides an online toolkit for developing a school-wide PBIS model at any school. The site gives an online manual, training guidelines, and presentations.

In the last few years, we have seen a devastating number of school shootings. On a weekly basis, we are reminded of the concerns and safety issues at our schools. One approach to prevention and intervention is developing a trauma-informed school model. This approach unites members of a school community—school resource officers, administrators, teachers, and staff. This model not only aids schools in responding to a crisis but also develops a school culture that fosters community and security. These traits empower and prepare schools to more effectively respond to the needs of students impacted by trauma (Treatment and Service Adaptive Center, n.d.).

This chapter provides an outline of trauma on children within school systems; describes the implication of a trauma-informed model of teachers, administrators, and parents; identifies tools that can be utilized in schools; and provides resources needed for a trauma-informed school.

REFERENCES

American Psychiatric Association. (2013). *Diagnostic and statistical manual of mental disorders* (5th ed.). Washington, DC: American Psychiatric Association.

Anderson, A. R., Christenson, S. L., Sinclair, M. F., & Lehr, C. A. (2004). Check and connect: The importance of relationships for promoting engagement with school. *Journal of School Psychology, 42*(2), 95–113.

Burke, N., Hellmana, J., Scott, B., Weemsb, C., & Carrion, V. (2011). The impact of adverse childhood experiences on an urban pediatric population. *Child Abuse & Neglect.* doi:10.1016/j.chiabu.2011.02.006

Center of Teacher Effectiveness. (n.d.). Time to teach. Retrieved from www.timetoteachtrainer.com.

McIntosh, K., Campbell, A., Carter, D., & Dickey, C. (2009). Differential effects of a tier 2 behavioral intervention based on function of problem behavior. *Journal of Positive Behavior Interventions, 11*(2), 82–93.

National Child Traumatic Stress Network Schools Committee. (2008, October). *Child trauma toolkit for educators.* Los Angeles, CA: National Center for Child Traumatic Stress.

Stein, B. D., Elliott, M. N., Tu, W., Jaycox, L. H., Kataoka, S. H., Wong, M., & Fink, A. (2003). "School-based intervention for children exposed to violence": Reply. *Journal of the American Medical Association, 290*(19): 2542.

Treatment and Service Adaptive Center. (n.d.). Trauma aware schools. Retrieved from https://traumaawareschools.org.

Wiest, C., & Lee, C. (2016). Trauma-informed schools. *Journal of Evidence-Informed Social Work, 13*(5).

Chapter 6

How Can We Develop an Infrastructure of Safe Schools?

Veronika Ospina-Kammerer

Creating safe schools can be accomplished by providing training for school administrators, teachers, staff, students, and their parents/families, as well as other professionals (e.g., counselors, social workers, school nurses, public safety officers, and others). Parental or caretaker involvement is paramount for focused strategies and successful outcome for any child. The overall goal is to provide a safe, peaceful environment for students where learning is an enjoyable process. Therefore, safe schools must focus on physical safety for students, violence prevention, mental health/wellness, and social/life skills.

RISK FACTORS

The accumulations of risk factors and opportunity in children's lives is important to consider. Research shows that very rarely does a single risk factor or a single opportunity factor account for much in the outcome of children. There is not one cause for a tragedy; there is only the accumulation of multiple risk factors that often creates a significant problem.

If children grow up without nurturing parents or caretakers, without a secure homelike environment, those children are more likely to act out with maladaptive behavior. The absence of a parent, parental neglect, drug abuse in a parent, mental illness in a parent, low educational attainment in a parent, child abuse in the family, and exposure to bullying in schools or in cyberspace are burdens on children's shoulders; he or she cannot stand up under the weight (Miller, Martin, & Schamess, 2003).

HOW TO RESPOND TO STUDENTS'
PSYCHOSOCIAL CRISIS

Based on prevention implications from school shooting research, cases of targeted school violence are not spontaneous, affect-driven acts resulting directly from the present situation but rather develop during an extended period of distress, deliberation, and planning. It is very important to recognize that almost all targeted school violence appears to be spurred by a personal, psychosocial crisis. Based on a series of German case studies and several international studies, the crisis itself could be compounded by stressful events that are closely linked to the motives for the violent acts, such as rejection by peers or conflicts with teachers.

Research findings point to the perpetrators' lack of ability to cope adequately with stressors because of emotional disturbances or mental disorders. People with inadequate coping skills often choose inappropriate ways to deal with their crisis and act on their despair, revenge, and anger. Moreover, the loss of attachment figures (parents, mentors, caretakers) adds to the personal psychosocial crisis. Filipp (1997) defined a psychosocial crisis as an event or situation that triggers a threat to identity, loss of orientation, blockade of aims, or retraumatization resulting from an acute overload of the individual's usual system of coping.

What are the observable warning behaviors parents, teachers, and caretakers must recognize? For instance, warning signs include verbal or written threats, leakage of violent intentions, preoccupation with violence and weapons, violent video games, or suicidal intentions. Leakage has been observed in most cases prior to the violent event. However, leakage does not necessarily lead to a violent act, but it is a red flag for any parent, teacher, or caretaker.

What kind of leaks are common and could create a psychosocial crisis? Students may talk about their violent intentions through boasting comments, letters, essay writings, media, tattoos, clothing, and any other form of self-expression that are out of the ordinary. Not every leakage leads to a violent act, but they need to be evaluated to prevent any catastrophic situation.

Schools are environments that can provide valuable opportunities for prevention and intervention because crisis symptoms and warning behavior become apparent. However, there are barriers in school systems and a culture that does not always allow systematic and open exchange of information—for example, a code of silence among students (individual and peer pressure); communication barriers with parents, teachers, staff, and law enforcement; nonverbal behavior does not get recognized (not recognizing clues); and students can fall through the cracks.

In 2017, the Networks Against School Shootings (NETWASS) program was funded by the Federal Ministry of Education and Research in Germany. As a result, the NETWASS program was developed (Leuschner et al., 2017; Scheithauer, Leuschner, & NETWASS Research Group, 2014) and a threat assessment approach derived in part from the Virginia Student Threat Assessment Guidelines (Cornell & Sheras, 2006).

The NETWASS program's focus is on teacher training and on networking with external partners rather than on school-based multidisciplinary teams. The NETWASS program puts a main focus on teacher training and on networking with external partners rather than on school-based multidisciplinary teams.

The NETWASS is a research-based and developmentally informed prevention program for schools. The core approach of the prevention model is the following:

- Identify a student experiencing a psychosocial crisis that could lead to violence.
- Evaluate possible warning behaviors reliably.
- Implement appropriate and supportive measures.
- Pass on the most serious cases to the Crisis Prevention Team (CPT).

OVERVIEW OF THE NETWASS PREVENTION MODEL FOR TARGETED SCHOOL VIOLENCE

First Stage: A student engaging in warning behavior or showing crisis symptoms that raise concern. If a warning behavior or crisis symptom cannot be explained by school staff, observations should be forwarded to a central prevention appointee to follow-up with more in-depth assessments of the student.

Second Stage: The prevention appointee is responsible for collecting further information about the student's situation from other sources (parents, members of school staff, official documents) and presenting the information to the Crisis Prevention Team (CPT).

Third Stage: This stage defines the core of the NETWASS crisis prevention model. The CPT consists of the prevention appointee, the school principal, specially trained members of the school staff, the school's social worker, and the homeroom teacher of the student concerned. Their task is to discuss all the available information with the purpose of answering the central questions:

- Is the student showing signs of a psychosocial crisis or warning behavior that could lead to violence?

• Does the student's overall situation reflect individual vulnerabilities and social strain factors?

The CPT will construct an intervention plan with appropriate interventions that will help the student to cope with the crisis and end a threatening situation.

Fourth Stage: The NETWASS crisis prevention model consists of case monitoring by one or more staff members to assure an effective and sustainable intervention. Staff members responsible for case monitoring provide feedback to the CPT whether measures have started, or ended, or were rejected, canceled, or require a new assessment by the CPT.

The NETWASS program is an effective prevention method for schools. The program requires only a moderate degree of staff training. It is important that readiness for change and willingness to engage in implementation efforts are key factors in preventing targeted school violence (Leuschner et al., 2017).

HOW TO PREVENT STUDENTS "FALLING THROUGH THE CRACKS"

Sharing of information about students who exhibit problem behavior, "red flags," or "clues" presents a challenge to school administrators, teachers, school counselors, social workers, and staff trying to both assist students in crisis and honor the Federal Educational Rights of Privacy Act (FERPA). According to research findings and law enforcement investigations, sharing of information is paramount and critical to the prevention of violence.

The adolescent "code of silence" can discourage teens from telling their parents or teachers about a classmate's plan to cause harm to him/herself and others. However, it is known that most attackers engaged in some behavior prior to the incident that indicated a need for help. In most all literature about school shooters, other people know about the shooter's behavior, safety threats, and weapon access, but avoided reporting it.

WHAT ARE THE SIGNS OF A SCHOOL SHOOTER?

Bondue and Scheithauer (2011) identified six warning signs for a school shooter:

1. planning the attack;
2. leaking the plan;

3. enjoying violent fantasies;
4. experiencing peer rejection and bullying;
5. experiencing a significant loss; and
6. facing a negative school climate.

School attacks are not spontaneous events; on the contrary, offenders plan often for many months in advance. Red flags emerge over a period of several weeks, months, and often years and in different settings and with different people.

Therefore, creating and promoting a culture of safety where students, teachers, and staff can share is key to prevention of violence. Most importantly, an information-sharing system or culture remains key to develop a positive school climate and the prevention of violence (Goodrum, Woodward, & Thompson, 2017).

School environment, teacher relationships, and student relationships are key factors of school safety. Some students report feeling less safe in undersupervised and crowded areas, and when feeling unsafe, school performance often suffers. Students prefer an authoritative climate consisting of clear expectations and predetermined consequences. Student support includes elements that bolster students' connectivity toward the school. The physical structure may also be an important component of school climate—for example, the degree to which the school is perceived as noisy/crowded or well maintained and cared for (Williams, Schneider, Wornell, & Langhinrichsen-Rohling, 2018).

Supportive strategies and examples for teachers and students include: social health, humor and laughter, expressive writing, poetry, prayer, positive self-talk; mindfulness, and meditation. Mental health/wellness and social/life skills are the pillars for crises interventions and preventions in schools and communities. How can we prevent crisis in schools and communities? Here are a few practical strategies to consider:

- safety that goes beyond high-tech security;
- gang and "outsider" awareness and prevention programs in schools and in communities;
- zero tolerance of bullying, harassment, or gang recruitments;
- faculty and school staff have open lines of communication and foster a wholesome sense of tolerance and respect;
- African saying "it takes a whole village to bring up children";
- working as a team with other agencies (courts, public assistance, housing authorities, etc.); and
- cooperation with city and county government agencies.

Overall, teachers, students/parents, and staff need to focus on:

- physical health (nutrition and sport);
- emotional health (approach life as an opportunity for being creative, happy, and helpful); and
- social health (interact in a manner that promotes the other's well-being as well as one's own well-being—that is, developing the characteristics of kindness, fairness, authenticity, gratitude, and open-mindedness).

MENTAL HEALTH/WELLNESS SKILLS ILLUSTRATIONS (ROTAN & OSPINA-KAMMERER, 2007)

Humor and Laughter

Humor is the quality of being laughable or comical. Laughter is the ability to express emotion. Laughter can be practiced by everyone. Laughter is universal; it has no cultural barrier, and it is practiced by all ethnic groups. There is no limit on time or when or how to laugh.

Expressive Writing

Expressive writing is the venting of emotions and cognitions through words and stories. Writing is a form of personal expression of the "self." For instance, a student or a teacher is living with the reality of being bullied, harassed, or treated unfairly, expressive writing could be a way of expressing certain feelings from dreams or daily experiences. Expressive writing could give this person a symbolic way of exploring his or her personal and cultural viewpoints. It could help students to express their emotions through words and symbols. It could create awareness and ways for teachers to assist students who are under emotional stress.

Poetry

Poetry creates images through word connection. Poetry is usually practiced by people who are interested in it. However, somebody does not need to know how to write poetry to use poetry. Poetry is universal, meaning different cultures use poetry in different ways. Poetry can be a very useful tool to help students, teachers, and staff to cope with difficult situations.

Prayer

Prayer is a request, expression of gratitude, or praise made to another. Many people who use prayer do have a religious faith or belief in a deity to whom they pray. A person's belief system is very important and can be of great comfort in daily living and during difficult times. Prayers can help a person who feels overwhelmed to restore a sense of order and hope.

Positive Self-Talk

Positive self-talk involves the positive words, sentences, and inner dialogue we use to label and interpret our thoughts, feelings, beliefs, and experiences. A person who uses positive thoughts and focuses on positive feelings and experiences is often able to influence his or her emotional and physical well-being. Teachers and staff can be great role models and motivators for positive thought processes in and outside the classroom.

Mindfulness

In mindfulness, you simply note any thoughts or feelings as they occur. You observe them intentionally without judgment moment by moment, allowing them to gently float away from you.

Meditation

Meditation involves a focused state of calmness and detached awareness. Meditation is not daydreaming or even imagery. It is not an altered state like hypnosis. The hallmark of meditation is being in the present moment. Meditation helps you to become relaxed—it brings about a physiological response called the relaxation response.

The other "power" in meditation is that it is a practice in letting go of thought and feeling and placing yourself in the here and now. Meditation can be done seated, standing, or walking (Ospina-Kammerer, 2012).

Safe schools can be ensured by focusing not only on technology but also on process and people such as to provide training for school administrators, teachers, staff, students, and their parents/families in regard to recognizing the accumulation of risk factors that do damage.

School administrators and professional teams should consider:

• developing an infrastructure of safer schools;
• assessing risk factors;
• responding to students' psychosocial crises;

- looking out for signs of a school shooter; and
- using focused and supportive strategies/interventions for teachers and students.

Parents, caretakers, and teachers are gaining the knowledge to recognize early on any psychosocial crisis to prevent any students from "falling through the cracks." Safety in schools can also be ensured by providing supportive strategies for teachers and students to increase their coping skills. Mental health/ wellness and social/life skills need to be practiced in every school.

REFERENCES

Bondue, R., & Scheithauer, H. (2011). Explaining and preventing school shootings: Chances and difficulties of control. In W. Heitmeyer, H-G. Haupt, S. Malthaner, & K. Kirschner (Eds.), *Control of violence* (pp. 295–314). New York: Springer.

Cornell, D. G., & Sheras, P. (2006). *Guidelines for responding to student threats of violence.* Longmont, CO: Sopris West.

Filipp, H. S. (1997). *Kritische Lebensereignisse [Critical life events].* Munich, Germany: Urban & Schwarzenberg.

Goodrum, S., Woodward, W., & Thompson, J. (2017). Sharing information to promote a culture of safety. *NASSP Bulletin, 101*(32), 215–240.

Leuschner, V., Fiedler, N., Schultze, M., Ahlig, N., Goebel, K., Sommer, F., Scholl, J., Cornell, D., & Scheithauer, H. (2017). Prevention of targeted school violence by responding to students' psychosocial crises: The NETWASS program. *Child Development, 88*(1), 68–82.

Machin, L. (2014). *Working with loss and grief.* Thousand Oaks, CA: Sage.

Miller, J., Martin, I. R., & Schamess, G. (2003). *School violence.* Denver, CO: Love Publishing.

Ospina-Kammerer, V. (2012). Meditation. In C. R. Figley (Ed.), *Encyclopedia of trauma: An interdisciplinary guide.* Thousand Oaks, CA: Sage.

Rotan, L., & Ospina-Kammerer, V. (2007). *MindBody medicine: Foundations and practical applications.* New York: Routledge.

Williams, S., Schneider, M., Wornell, C., & Langhinrichsen-Rohling, J. (2018). Students' perceptions of school safety: It is not just about being bullied. *The Journal of School Nursing, 34*(4), 319–330.

Chapter 7

Animal Support Therapies

Rhondda Waddell and Debra Mims

This chapter describes the use of animals in educational settings for safety and therapeutic purposes and explores the student benefits of animals in educational settings. Policy guidelines and safety issues regarding the use of animals in the school and classroom settings are also discussed.

CASE SCENARIO

Carol Johnson was a happy twenty-eight-year-old female passionate about teaching high school American history. Yet, sadly she has become a part of the history of classroom gun violence in America as a result of a recent shoot-out that ended in multiple deaths of students and teachers at her school. She was teaching about the riots and unrest of the civil rights movement, when gun shots were heard blasting outside of her classroom door. Moments turned into an eternity for her as the adolescent gunman riddled the door with holes, killing several students and wounding several others in a random act of violence.

She and other students survived the assault, yet many others did not throughout the schoolyard. In an attempt to solve the problem of school gun violence, politicians quickly recommended that teachers be allowed to be armed in an effort to defend themselves and their students from such harm. The American president in office, in the immediate aftermath of the shooting, encouraged that teachers be armed, as he stated, "They can fire out of love" (Trischitta, 2018).

Carol responded emphatically that she opposed the idea of bringing more guns into schools; she said that "dogs not guns in schools" was a better solution. Carol explained that a handgun would be no match for a machine gun, and that prevention was the best intervention.

She stated that she would embrace the idea of having a therapy dog in her classroom. During a town hall meeting many students explained they were afraid to come back to their class, but when Carol suggested the idea of having a therapy dog come to class, many quickly changed their minds.

Therapy dogs had been involved in the aftermath of the shooting, and had already begun to bond with the traumatized teachers, students, and grieving parents who had lost their children. Carol now waits to hear from school officials if a therapy dog in the classroom can be made a reality, offering increased security and sensitivity to all trying to cope with school gun violence.

The details of this case scenario are fictitious but are based on a true case involving a recent school shooting where numerous teacher and student lives were lost. The need for increased strategies to be developed to include animals to serve and protect public schools from gun violence is imminent.

John Dewey, Montessori, Piaget, Erickson, and Vygotsky all espoused using animals to teach children responsibility and in curriculum planning developing other skills like learning by doing and reflection (Fine, 2015). Educators recognize the value of including animals in the classroom as a way of meeting developmental and educational goals, helping students deepen their knowledge, skills, and interest in learning, and as a means of finding comfort when lacking motivation and when under stress.

More commonly, classrooms present challenges more than learning the educational materials, as children encounter external threats such as drugs and violence that infiltrate the lives of many children in America. More than ever animals provide comfort and protection.

Historically, prehistoric humans would not have survived the harsh conditions they faced on a daily basis struggling to survive in harsh conditions, and today's world is no different.

In the times we live in, where mental health stressors are challenging children's lives and their family members and often are resulting in depression, anxiety, and feelings of hopelessness, frequently the animal-assisted therapy provided by our best friends with fur and four legs is the main line of support for many.

This section seeks to discuss the benefits and challenges when animals are included in the educational setting. The use of animal-assisted therapy (AAT) and animal-assisted activity (AAA) provides a useful tool that could be offered in varied educational settings and particularly in school counseling programs.

The time has come to recognize that the human-animal bond is valuable to us all and will help us stay connected to each other on a deeper level, reducing the potential for violence and the escalation of fear. Animals have been noted to make important contributions to the education of students. Many of these animals are used for therapeutic purposes.

Often animals are used for teaching humane education principles that encourage respect for living things, and for enhancing students' personal, social, and moral development. Additionally, animal-assisted programs with students are becoming increasingly popular in school and therapeutic settings on a regular basis.

Research that examines children's interactions with animals has demonstrated marked benefits for children physiologically (Odendall, 2000), emotionally, socially (Anderson & Olson, 2006; Walters, Esteves, & Stokes; Zasloff & Hart, 1999), and physically (Gee et al., 2007). The presence of a dog has been found to lower behavioral, emotional, and verbal distress in children when participating in a mildly stressful activity (Nagengast et al., 1997), and lower blood pressure and heart rate when a child reads aloud (Friedmann et al., 1983).

Dogs in particular have been found to contribute to elementary students' overall emotional stability and to more positive attitudes toward school in children diagnosed with severe emotional disorders (Anderson & Olson, 2006). The list of research studies is extensive in regard to the benefits animals offer students in both therapeutic and educational settings in multi-disciplinary fields and is worthy of our close attention (Jalongo, 2006).

It is important to recognize that there are many different types of therapy animals, and they are used in a variety of educational settings. The most common are dogs, cats, and horses. Farm animals can be therapeutic as well as smaller or less common types of animals; rabbits, birds, fish, hamsters, and even llamas are increasingly seen in schools across America. Each of these animals have unique skills and make a contribution toward the educational and therapeutic process in which they are used.

There can be many benefits to integrating AAT and AAA in the school setting. Careful planning is needed to align the animals with specific goals and objectives that are to be intentionally used in the classroom setting for educational or therapeutic purposes.

A list of common usages provided by the Delta organization in 1999 includes: gaining knowledge about animals; learning humane animal care; increasing motor and physical skill development through human-animal interactions; practicing animal training and discipline skills; learning about kindness, responsibility, and compassion; and experiencing the human-animal bond. Another significant use of animal-assisted therapy may be to curb violence in schools. Animals in classrooms have empirically been proven to enhance humane attitudes toward animals and these more humane attitudes persisted in a one-year follow up (Ascione & Weber, 1999). This same study showed a generalization from humane attitudes toward animals to human-directed empathy. This suggests strongly that emotional connections made with animals can transfer to more empathetic attitudes toward other persons.

IMPLICATIONS OF ANIMALS IN
SCHOOLS FOR STUDENTS

Dogs not only can be therapeutic in animal-assisted therapy but can also detect prescription drugs, alcohol, guns, and explosives without having to open bags, lockers, or cars. Students in a Michigan school district responded that they felt safer thanks to dogs that regularly searched schools for weapons and illegal substances (DeNisco, 2014). The financial cost of having a monthly sniffer dog visit a school was quoted to be about $5,000 per year; however, some schools are provided this service free by law enforcement and their K-9 units.

Most schools that deploy such canine units report a decline in violators when dogs are used for detection of drugs, guns, and weapons. Students have varied responses to canine searches with most students expressing that they feel safer and enjoy the presence of having the dogs on campus. There is also a network of dog handlers nationwide who are willing to provide canine services, and dog trainers are growing in numbers who help to keep an ongoing supply of such trained dogs available for service.

Not all students like to have dogs sniffing around in their personal property for a number of reasons reported. One key identified problem is that some dogs are not very effective at targeting only drug possessors or specified items on the list to be searched. Several studies have identified that drug dogs are prone to false alerts, which then lead to unjustified search and the student's embarrassment. Records of drug-sniffing dogs in one Washington school district indicated that dogs were incorrect 85 percent of the times they alerted to a substance (Sullivan, 2011).

While some people have expressed concern that in actuality drug-sniffing dogs are frequently influenced by the dog handler's racial biases, there are more benign explanations too, such as the dog being inherently unreliable in the detection skill level. This leads to serious complications for schools to incorporate animals into educational settings requiring specific implication procedures (NSW Department of Education, 2018).

IMPLICATIONS OF ANIMALS IN SCHOOLS
FOR SCHOOL ADMINISTRATORS

While the use of dogs as therapy animals and safety patrols vary in support by students as described, in Los Angeles some say school safety hinges on guns, cameras, or alarms in classrooms; Officer Mark Gomer and Kristi Schiller think especially trained dogs take point in preventing violence. Gomer, who has trained about eight thousand dogs over twenty years and has three children in the public school district, states, "These canines are extremely social, yet highly qualified warriors that are accustomed to going straight to the source of a threat or shooter and disengaging the suspect armed with a weapon," reported Schiller (Manning, 2013).

As a result of a low number of campus police or sufficient law enforcement agencies that can service schools around the country, Schiller is looking to provide a new support business called K9s4KIDs where she will provide canines free of charge to schools. If a school applies for and is chosen to receive a dog, it will be fully trained and paid for through her organization. A typical cost of a dog that is fully trained ranges between $10,000 and $15,000.

The Health and Safety Work Act of 1974 places a duty on employers to safeguard the health, safety, and welfare at work of teachers, pupils, and visitors. This includes an obligation to minimize the risk of the transfer of disease from animals to people. Schools should satisfy themselves that animals are to be sourced from reputable providers, that they are kept in a good state of health, and that suitable hygiene precautions are followed by anyone coming into contact with the animals. Sick animals should be isolated and advice sought from a veterinary physician on how to best care for the animal (NUT, 2001).

The school would decide who would be the dog's handler, and provide ongoing support of the dog's care. This expense would entail medical care, food, a forever home, and the handler willing to be responsible for the dog daily. School officials have to recognize that other considerations would need to be thought through as well, beginning with possible health problems the dog or students alike may have with regard to having an animal in the school setting, and how and if the dog might cause an unnecessary distraction in the classroom, for starters.

Once the school has decided to have the addition of an animal on their premises for either school safety or AAT purposes, then the responsibility to ensure the provision of adequate resources and facilities for the appropriate care of the animal must be determined. The afterhours care of the animals must be considered to include evenings, nights, and weekends. Certainly emergency plans must be put in place to make sure that the dog is offered safe care during a natural disaster or other threat to their safety. A plan to offer a grievance procedure in writing must be drafted to allow for any animal-related complaints to be processed fairly and quickly.

The school leaders, such as the principal, must be willing to comply with relevant legislation and laws set to provide guidelines on having animals in school settings. All legal and required documentation under the animal welfare act and state laws must be maintained and available for inspection. The animal welfare liaison officer is to be the principal of the school in an elementary setting, or appointed by the principal, and responsible for meeting all the requirements relevant to legislation, animal care standards, and the monitoring of programs for compliance when animals are involved in the school setting.

IMPLICATIONS OF ANIMALS IN SCHOOLS FOR TEACHERS

Teachers like Carol Johnson in our case scenario work hard every day to educate our nations' children, yet the unthinkable can happen at any given moment to end their lives due to gun violence in the schools. Carol recognized in the aftermath of a horrendous school shooting the value of AAT to offer the necessary unconditional love and support that was so desperately needed in this strained time of grief.

It was Carol's best instinct to reach out to the school officials for that very support that would allow herself and students to return to the classroom with more comfort and security than they had previously. You might say that animals are "the pack that have the back" of the schools' human companions they connect with when given a chance. Once an animal enters the classroom setting, the teacher is ultimately responsible for achieving the educational goals that animal is set to provide, and to make sure care of that animal is provided at all times.

Again like the other school leaders the teacher must be appraised and abide by the legislative rules and laws that provide guidelines for animals in educational settings. The teacher needs to understand the animal's needs and comply with them regarding the physical, behavioral, and social care requirements of different species.

The students must be informed, as well, in how to respond to each animal's needs and comply with these with respect to their different personalities and age requirements. This includes requiring approval forms to be administered and completed from school officials, students, and parents with regard to having the animal in the classroom setting. It also includes the care of the animal, and it is the responsibility of the teacher to make certain to alleviate any pain, distress, harm, or illness at all times for the animals located in the educational setting. Lastly, if there is loss of the animal's life, the teacher is responsible for the proper disposal of the animal immediately.

In addition to managing the needs of the students and the animals, the teacher is also responsible for delivering the educational curricula. Many questions should be considered to fully implement the animal into the educational setting, such as:

1. What are the key educational goals that will be achieved through the presence of an animal in the classroom?
2. What and how do the curricula support that goal?
3. What are the specific academic learning outcomes and how can the animal play a role in achieving those outcomes? (Fine, 2015)

IMPLICATIONS OF ANIMALS IN SCHOOLS FOR PARENTS

Special concerns for some parents are absolutely recognized as essential in that the safety of students and everyone in the program with animals in attendance is paramount. The primary concern for most parents for their student involved with animals is that cleanliness and allergies are deterrents to animals use in educational settings.

In one study it was determined that only 6 percent of people seen by allergists in North America have an allergic reaction as a result of animal dander (Elliot et al., 1985). Selecting an animal that does not shed, that is bathed and groomed regularly, and that is vaccinated routinely before classroom visitation occurs significantly reduces dander, minimizing potential allergies. Proper handwashing is highly recommended and in severe cases of allergies the animal must not be touched by the student and distance should be maintained to prevent an outbreak of the allergic reaction.

Another common parental concern in having animals in the educational setting involves safety issues for students (Jalongo, 2008). Dog bites are more common among very young children, but can be prevented with proper age-appropriate lessons and proper handling of the animal. Students need to be taught to be gentle and appropriately approach an animal, learn how to play nicely with animals, and how to act if the student is fearful of the animal.

The concerns of parents should be respected and dealt with early on to address any issues and decide on agreed-upon procedures of how to begin a program that incorporates animals in an educational setting. Cultural difference where some believe that animals are "unclean" and disease carriers should be avoided with regard to the use of animals in the educational setting for everyone's sake including the animal. Some school districts lack clear policies regarding animals being allowed in the educational setting, and others have a clear "no animals allowed" policy. Clearly there is a need for clarification and understanding of how to provide safe and useful animal support in schools. The parents must be willing to allow their children to engage with the animal before an AAT or school safety animal is brought on the premises.

IMPLICATIONS OF ANIMALS IN SCHOOLS FOR SUPPORT STAFF (COUNSELORS, SOCIAL WORKERS, SCHOOL AIDES, SROS)

Trained therapy dogs, farm animals, and other small animals are being used more often in the educational setting. Animals in an educational setting provide improved socialization and communication, reduce isolation and loneliness, brighten the mood of students, improve recall and memory, relieve stress and grief symptoms, and improve self-esteem. Animals help with reading programs, help with mobility strengthening for the mobile impaired, and teach students multiple educational concepts found in science classes.

Animal-assisted therapy programs with horse riding programs (hippotherapy) and programs designed to facilitate interaction between children and dolphins are subject to further scrutiny and supervision. Research exploring AAT programs with horses indicates that horses may offer a variety of benefits for students in need of increased flexible movement, balance, gross motor condition, and cardiovascular function, as well as speech and language abilities (Granger & Kogan, 2006; Maculey & Gutierrez, 2004).

However, the drawback for large animals such as horses, farm animals, and dolphins include having the proper environment to support the animal, housing, feeding, and the provision of veterinary care for them. Also, if these animals are kept off campus the cost of transporting students to stables and aquariums are logistical concerns and expense. These large animals also may pose more risk to the safety of a student based on their size primarily.

Animals have long been incorporated into classroom settings as a way of meeting the developmental and educational goals of students (Uttley, 2013). It is important that school officials, teachers, staff supports, students, and parents work together to bring animals into the educational setting through clear and well-planned procedures to ensure the best outcome for the humans and animals involved.

Research has shown that animals in a classroom environment can be a valuable teaching tool for children (National Academy of Sciences, 2004).

Using animals in a prudent and sensible method can provide an excellent way to motivate and encourage children to learn. Additionally, the conscientious use of animals in a classroom environment can foster empathy, patience, and compassion for another living creature while encouraging humane treatment in establishing the human-animal bond (National Academy of Sciences, 2004).

Humane interaction, responsibility, and respect for animals can be taught judiciously to children as young as preschool. Through guidance, proper supervision, and the utilization of live demonstrations and humane interaction, teachers can motivate and instill the love of learning about animal husbandry and ethical care of animals (Daly & Suggs, 2010; Zasloff, Hart, & DeArmond, 1999).

Studies have shown that bonding with an animal in the classroom has helped children who have not had the opportunity to own or socialize with an animal be able to express their emotions of affection while also helping to increase the child's vocabulary and communication development and enriching the overall classroom environment (Zasloff, Hart, & DeArmond, 1999). Research on human-animal interactions by Gee, Griffin, and McCardle (2017) has shown the indirect effects associated with an animal in the classroom as improving a child's attention, motivation, engagement, and cognitive development.

Animals such as fish, hamsters, or turtles have been utilized by teachers in the classroom to help calm and de-stress the learning environment. Children with developmental challenges and behavioral and learning disabilities have been able to calm themselves and relax by looking at fish swimming in a tank or observing the interaction of hamsters or turtles (Ganzert & McCullough, 2015).

A 2015 study by American Humane Association researchers found that sensible and sagacious use of animals in the classroom environment enhanced academic performance and increased the use of pro-social behavior and social skills among students. Educators have learned to use animals as a way to both augment and enrich the learning environment while also providing an unconditional, nonjudgmental atmosphere in which to engage with peers (National Academy of Sciences, 2004).

Animal-assisted programs have the potential to broaden the ways in which individuals view the role of animals by exposing children to new and different concepts while also helping to alleviate any fears, preconceptions, or biases associated with animals. Carol Johnson from our case scenario reminds us of the value that AAT can provide to students and faculty alike.

Carol intuitively recognized that animals are perceived to be non-judgmental participants who are separate from the complexities found in human relationships, and that they offer a valuable form of social and emotional comfort in educational settings. Given appropriately guided activities in a structured situation and praise for humane interaction with animals, children can be taught responsibility, compassion, empathy, and respect for all living things.

Animals give back and have our backs, which cannot help but to positively influence the well-being and knowledge base of all who encounter them in the educational setting.

The ideas presented in this chapter offer opportunities to integrate best practices in mental health considerations into school safety plans and discussions. There is not one best thing for all, but many options for school administrators and police authorities to consider in addition to traditional variables of school safety.

Reed (2018) identified the need for protecting students' mental health in schools. He pointed out the need to address the negative impact school shootings have on students. The National Child Traumatic Stress Network published a guide for talking to children about a school shooting (www.NCTSN.org). Resources such as this checklist can assist teachers, administrators, staff, parents, and community leaders in the aftermath of a school shooting.

REFERENCES

Arkow, P. (2011). The impact of companion animals on social capital and community violence: Setting research, policy and program agendas. *Journal of Sociology & Social Welfare, XL*(4), 33–56.

Arkow, P. (2013). *Animal-assisted therapy and activities: A study and research resource guide for the use of companion animals in animal-assisted interventions.* Stratfort, NJ: AnimalTherapy.net.

Beetz, A., Uynas-Moberg, K., Julius, H., & Kotrschal, K. (2012). Psychosocial and psychophysiological effects of human-animal interactions: The possible role of oxytocin. *Front Psychology, 3*, 234. doi:10.3389/fpsyg.2012.00234

Bryant, B. (2008, September 30–October 2). *Social support in relation to human animal interaction.* Bethesda, MD: Paper presented at the NICHD/Mars meeting on Directions in Human-Animal Interaction Research: Child Development, Health and Therapeutic Interventions.

Chandler, C. (2012). *Animal assisted therapy in counseling* (2nd edition). New York: Taylor & Francis.

Fine, A. (2010). Understanding our kinship with animals. In *Handbook on animal-assisted therapy: Theoretical foundations and guidelines for practice* (3rd edition). doi:10.1016/B978-0-12-381453-1.10001-7

Fine, A., & Mackintosh, T. (2016). Animal-assisted interventions: Entering a crossroads of explaining an instinctive bond under the scrutiny of scientific inquiry. *Encyclopedia of Mental Health* (2), 68–73. doi:10.1016/B978-0-12-397045-9.00120-8

Friesen, L. (2010). Exploring animal-assisted programs with children in school and therapeutic contexts. *Early Childhood Education Journal, 37*(4), 261–267. doi:10.1007/s10643-009-0349-5

Kruger, K., & Serpell, J. (2010). Animal-assisted interventions in mental health: Definitions and theoretical foundations. In A. H. Fine (Ed.), *Handbook of animal-assisted therapy: Theoretical foundations and guidelines for practice* (3rd edition) (pp. 33–48). San Diego, CA: Academic Press. doi:10.1016/B978-0-12-381453-1.10003-0

Marcus, D. (2013). The science behind animal-assisted therapy. *Current Pain & Headache Reports, 17*(4), 1. doi:10.1007/s11916-013-0322-2

Marino, L. (2012). Construct validity of animal-assisted therapy: How important is the animal in AAT? *Anthrozoos, 25,* 139–151. doi:10.2752/1753037 12X13353430377219

McCardle, P., McCune, S., Griffin, J., Esposito, L., & Freund, L. (2011). *Animals in our lives: Human-animal interaction in family, community, and therapeutic settings.* Baltimore: Paul H. Brooks.

Odendaal, J. (2000). Animal-assisted therapy-magic or medicine? *Journal of Psychosomatic Research, 49*(4), 275–280. doi:10.1016/S0022-3999(00)

O'Haire, M. (2010). Companion animals and human health: Benefits, challenges, and the road ahead. *Journal of Veterinary Behavior, 5,* 226–234. doi:10.1016/j.veb.2010.02.002

Simon, V. A., Feiring, C., & McElroy, S. K. (2010). Making meaning of traumatic events: Youths' strategies for processing childhood sexual abuse are associated with psychosocial adjustment. *Child Maltreatment, 15,* 229–241. doi:10.1177/1077559510370365

Stevens, N., Gerhart, J., Goldsmith, R., Heath, N., Chesney, S., & Hobfoll, S. (2013). Emotion regulation difficulties, low social support, and interpersonal violence mediate the link between childhood abuse and posttraumatic stress symptoms. *Behavior Therapy, 44,* 152–161. doi:10.1016/j.beth.2012.09.003

Wells, D. (2009). The effects of animals on human health and well-being. *Journal of Social Issues, 65,* 523–543. doi: 10.1111/j.1540-4560.2009.01612.x

RESOURCES

Animal*learn*: www.animalearn.org/studentCenter.php#.VETVPPk_C_E

Association for School Curriculum and Development (school crisis intervention model): www.ascd.org/publications/educational-leadership/nov94/vol52/num03/School-Crisis- Response@-Expecting-the-Unexpected.aspx

CDC: www.cdc/features/animalsinschools
HOPE Animal-Assisted Crisis Response: www.hopeaacr.org (children and adults)
HOPE Animal-Assisted Crisis Response is a national all-volunteer, non-profit, crisis response organization with specially trained handlers (psychological first aid, incident command, etc.) and canines trained and tested for crisis response work. Agencies call upon HOPE AACR teams to provide comfort and support to people affected by disasters. Scientific evidence has shown animals are a positive factor in helping people cope with traumatic events. HOPE AACR teams are educated to be effective and professional while working in stressful, unpredictable environments.
HSUS: www.humanesociety.rog/parents_educators/classroom_pet.html
Institute for Humane Education: http://humaneeducation.org
Latham Foundation: www.Latham.org/research-and-resources
National Center for Emotional Wellness (school crisis management checklist): www.nationalcenterforemotionalwellness.org/school-crisis-management-checklist
RedRover: https://redrover.org/resource/animal-response-teams
RedRover staff and volunteers provide temporary emergency sheltering, resources, financial assistance, and emotional support when animals and people are in crisis. We empower educators to help kids develop empathy and awareness of animals' well-being and increase awareness about the importance of the human-animal bond.
The Tampa Bay Regional Critical Incident Team: https://tbrcit.org
The Tampa Bay Regional Critical Incident Team, Inc. (TBRCIT) 501(C)(3) was organized in 1986 to offer first responders/emergency service workers in the Tampa Bay area a comprehensive, multi-component, peer-driven, organized crisis intervention response for the reduction and control of the harmful aspects of stress as a result of a critical incident.

Chapter 8

School Safety Policies, Politics, and Advocacy

Fern Aefsky

Previous chapters discussed the topics of police authority, educators, and mental health professionals and identified specific strategies that schools should consider and use in developing and implementing aspects of school safety plans. Briefly mentioned throughout the book is the need for policies and resources to support the work of schools with community stakeholders. This chapter will address how policy advocacy impacts all issues regarding school safety and how each constituent and group of constituents must insist on the ongoing focus for schools.

A major component of all school districts is the legal requirement for schools to have board policies. Those policies must be reviewed annually, and updated as needed. While this board function is a major responsibility of each school board, it has become a task that lawyers, school board members, and superintendents complete in a manner that seems rote. Unless a significant change is warranted due to a regulatory change or a circumstance, little emphasis is focused on this important task.

Board policies are public documents. If you look at many districts' policies, each is a page or so long and gives some specificity to policies. These broad guidelines need to be reviewed with sincerity, and focus on school safety is required by all districts.

In reviewing over twenty districts' policies from across the country in multiple states, there were few specific policies on school safety. Rather, specific policies regarding weapons, student discipline, expulsion are individually specified. While these meet the rules and regulations, it is time for school board policies to be inclusive of a broader approach to ensuring safe schools.

School leaders are charged with developing plans that are commensurate with laws and regulations of the state the school districts are located within. For example, New York—under Section 2801 of Title 2, Article 55—requires every district's school board to have a policy that requires district-wide safety plans, developed by district safety teams, and must include:

- policies and procedures for responding to implied or direct threats of violence, and acts of violence, by students, personnel, or visitors to the school;
- appropriate prevention and intervention strategies, such as
  - collaborative plans with police authorities designed so that school resource officers and other security personnel are trained, including in crisis intervention and de-escalation techniques;
- peer mediation and nonviolent conflict-resolution training programs;
- policies and procedures for annual safety training for staff and students, including violence prevention and mental health; and
- policies and procedures related to school building security.

California has established comprehensive school safety plan requirements under the Education Code, sections 32280–32289. Those requirements include:

- a school site team, made up of principal/designee, teacher, parent, and other staff members;
- an assessment of current status (annually) of school crime and school related incidents of violence;
- teacher notification of dangerous student procedures;
- procedures and policies for dealing with discipline, suspensions, and code of conduct; and
- schools are "encouraged" to include clear guidelines for mental health professionals and counselors "if used by the district."

In Texas, the governor shared a plan to change state policies and school safety recommendations after ten people were killed in a high school in Texas in May 2018. The core of the proposal is the need to add police officers and marshals to all school campuses. All recommendations in his plan are directed to:

- more police presence in schools;
- requirements of an expanded school safety and security committee, inclusive of community members, school members, and police authorities;
- expansion of mental health screening tool implementation to identified students from school counselors and trained school staff;
- mental health training for school personnel, inclusive of skills to identify signs of mental distress;
- improved gun safety measures; and
- emergency and active shooter training.

In Florida, the governor expedited a new school safety law after the Parkland shooting.

The law requires sworn law enforcement officers in every school in the state. The law designated $162 million to help schools meet that requirement, as well as an additional $99 million for districts to address specific safety needs in their schools.

The states mentioned are examples of what is occurring across the United States. School boards pass policies commensurate with new laws; legislatures pass new laws in urgency as a reaction to recent school shootings; politicians make statements about results. However, the political and bureaucratic response is only one part of the challenge. Once these aspects of change occur, what is the reality at the school-district levels?

State superintendents and national organizations of educational leaders have all identified a significant lack of resources to implement these new laws and policies. In Florida, the Association of District School Superintendents requested the funding that would enable them to implement the rule without reducing faculty, staff, or educational resources. While the amount of funding announced sounded like that is exactly what those monies ($261 million) allocated would do, the reality is that it may not be enough money to put resource officers in every school.

Another piece of that legislation passed and funds allocated (an additional $139 million) provides funding to districts to train some school staff, including teachers, to carry and use guns in schools. Many of the state's sixty-seven school districts have specifically stated that that is not a solution they are interested in pursuing.

In New York, a group of seventy-seven district superintendents from the Lower Hudson Valley called for allocation of funds for preventative measures and stricter gun laws as a way to ensure safer schools (Sanchez, 2018). Policy reforms they suggest include:

Non Sequitur by Wiley Miller

Figure 8.1.

- government funding to schools and communities for resources for prevention, support, and response from mental health professionals;
- facility funds for districts to upgrade safety measures and pay for safety audits;
- funding community agencies for mental health programs and youth programs;
- ban assault weapons from general ownership; and
- require thorough background check for all purchases of guns.

While these initiatives are worthy, they all seemingly stop short in a few ways for practitioners. In addition to the issues of funding and the need for mental health prevention and support, the need to engage others in collaboration for advocacy for safe schools is something all school communities should be addressing.

Schools have built-in partners who can be further engaged. Most schools have a parent organization (PTAs, PTOs), school advisory councils, business partnerships (internship providers, presenters at school events), booster clubs for music and sports, other club participants, prom committees, and parent university programs. These are just a few examples of groups that can be encouraged and invited to participate in matters of school safety.

Everyone needs to know that all schools have district safety plans and that they are public documents. However, emergency response plans must be confidential. Groups can inquire about their existence and ask if they are updated annually.

Having police or armed guards on campus is at the discretion of school districts. The idea of arming teachers is a national debate. Many states are considering legislation regarding guns on school campuses. The issue is one for both university and PK–12 campuses, and the debate is ongoing.

Research supports that increased gun access increases the possibility of more violence, not less (Rajan et al., 2017). Arming teachers is not a solution. Increasing support services in schools and community settings is a proactive way to address violent behavior among students. Stewart (2018) discussed research that determined that more guns in schools make them less safe, and resulted in more gun deaths and assaults. Students have found guns in schools where teachers were allowed to carry, teachers have accidently shot themselves, and the presence of guns creates a climate of fear.

There are no simple solutions to ensure safe schools. There are measures that can be taken, and communication is key. The following pages provide some resources for school leaders to consider when creating school safety plans.

SCHOOL BOARDS

A sample policy and resolution for school boards to implement from the California School Boards Association (www.csba.org):

School Safety Resolution

WHEREAS, our public schools are charged not only with supporting student achievement, but also providing a foundation for mental and physical health, personal growth, and civic engagement; and

WHEREAS, student safety is a prerequisite for consistently high levels of academic and social development; and

WHEREAS, violence and harassment can not only alienate students from their peers and their environment, thereby impeding learning, but also cause injuries and fatalities; and

WHEREAS, in its May 2017 study, *Indicators of School Crime and Safety: 2016*, the National Center for Education Statistics found that 21 percent of students aged 12 to 18 said they were bullied at school; and

WHEREAS, in the same study, 16 percent of high school students reported carrying a weapon at any point during the previous 30 days and 4 percent reported carrying a weapon on campus during the previous 30 days; and

WHEREAS, the study also noted that 4 percent of students had access to a loaded gun without adult permission, either at school or away from school, during the school year; and

WHEREAS, the horrific prospect of school shootings made an indelible impression on the national consciousness with the Columbine massacre of 1999; and

WHEREAS, more than 150,000 Americans have experienced a shooting on campus since the Columbine tragedy and hundreds of lives have been lost as a result; and

WHEREAS, gun violence on school campuses, while relatively rare, represents a particularly egregious and unacceptable threat to the lives of students, teachers, and staff across the country; and

WHEREAS, the recent massacre at Parkland, Florida, Marjory Stoneman Douglas High School took 17 lives and shocked the conscience of the nation; and

WHEREAS, gun violence in schools occurs in America with a frequency and a severity that is unparalleled anywhere in the world; and

WHEREAS, exposure to trauma can adversely affect a child's health for the rest of that child's life; and

WHEREAS, **[NAME OF SCHOOL DISTRICT, COUNTY BOARD OF EDUCATION OR ORGANIZATION]**, supports the right of students and staff to attend schools that are safe and free from violence and harassment, especially life-threatening forms of violence; and

WHEREAS, all students, regardless of background, deserve access to services that support and enhance their physical, mental, and emotional health; and

WHEREAS, safe schools provide an environment where teaching and learning can flourish; disruptions are minimized; violence, bullying, and fear are absent; students are not discriminated against; expectations for behavior are clearly communicated and standards of behavior are maintained; and consequences for infractions are consistently and fairly applied; and

WHEREAS, the most effective approach to creating safe school environments is a comprehensive, coordinated effort including schoolwide, districtwide and communitywide strategies supplemented with legislation, resources, and support at the state and federal legislation level;

NOW, THEREFORE BE IT RESOLVED, that the governing board of the **[NAME OF SCHOOL DISTRICT, COUNTY BOARD OF EDUCATION OR ORGANIZATION]**, has completed and holds regular drills as prescribed in both school site and district emergency plans and that said plans involve all school district personnel, law enforcement, fire and medical rescue personnel, emergency management personnel, and others essential to preventing, mitigating, or resolving any potential crisis.

BE IT FURTHER RESOLVED, that **[NAME OF SCHOOL DISTRICT, COUNTY BOARD OF EDUCATION OR ORGANIZATION]**, reviews school site discipline rules and procedures to ensure they are appropriately enforced and that student handbooks explaining codes of conduct, unacceptable behavior and disciplinary consequences are given to all students, parents, and caregivers.

BE IT FURTHER RESOLVED, that **[NAME OF SCHOOL DISTRICT, COUNTY BOARD OF EDUCATION OR ORGANIZATION]**, will continue to work with a broad spectrum of local community stakeholders, local law enforcement, mental health professionals, parents, students, teachers, and staff to take any threats of violence seriously and to develop, implement, and monitor policies and programs that foster and support a positive school climate, free from harassment and violence.

BE IT FURTHER RESOLVED, that **[NAME OF SCHOOL DISTRICT, COUNTY BOARD OF EDUCATION OR ORGANIZATION]**, urges the state of California and the United States Congress to invest in wraparound services to prevent bullying, harassment, discrimination, and violence in our schools and to provide funding for programs and staff such as counselors, nurses, and psychologists, that support students' mental, physical, and emotional health.

BE IT FURTHER RESOLVED, that **[NAME OF SCHOOL DISTRICT, COUNTY BOARD OF EDUCATION OR ORGANIZATION]**, asks the United States Congress to pass specific legislation that reduces the risk and severity of gun violence on school campuses and repeals the prohibition against data collection and research on gun violence by the U.S. Center for Disease Control (CDC).

BE IT FURTHER RESOLVED, that **[NAME OF SCHOOL DISTRICT, COUNTY BOARD OF EDUCATION OR ORGANIZATION]**, urges the state of California and the United States Congress to implement commonsense measures that prioritize student safety and environments where all students have the opportunity to learn, grow and thrive.

Adopted this_____ day of the month of_____in 2018.

Here are suggestions for board advocacy that school leaders can facilitate (from www.standforyourmission.org):

- Board members have the opportunity to be advocates for their organization and members of the organization.
- As a board member, a commitment is to support and strengthen the organization, reach goals, and support leadership in reaching those goals.
- Internal and external influence is strengthened by the board's ability to influence policy and legislation.
- Engaging others, both inside the school community and in concert with other school communities, matters.
- Ask the question: Who can we talk to, write to, to further our mission?

Additional considerations for advocating for public policy from the National Council of Nonprofits (www.councilofnonprofits.org):

- Identify one board member to lead a subcommittee on advocacy and public policy.
- Keep the item on every board agenda.
- Engage other stakeholders on the subcommittee: administrators, teachers, staff, students, parents, and community partners.
- Identify the key external figures: government officials, and politicians that can be targeted for lobbying.
- Contact other school districts to see if issues can be addressed by cohorts.
- Develop an annual plan for advocacy.

In developing a plan, here is a policy checklist that may assist in that process, developed by the Council of Chief School Officers (www.ccsso.org):

1. What is the problem you are trying to address?
2. What do you think is the cause of that problem?
3. What do you think are solutions to that problem?

(Remember, these pertain to an existing policy or the need for a policy to be developed.)

4. Is it a local, state, or federal policy?
5. Those impacted most by the policy—do they agree that it is a problem that needs a solution?
   a. Superintendents ___yes ___no
   b. Principals ___yes ___no
   c. Teachers ___yes ___no

    d. Parents ___yes ___no
    e. Students ___yes ___no
    f. Community members ___yes ___no
6. Has an implementation plan been developed? ___yes ___no
    a. Timeline specified? ___yes ___no
    b. Roles and responsibilities defined? ___yes ___no
    c. Communication process defined? ___yes ___no
7. Would a new or revised policy
    a. Create something positive? ___yes ___no
    b. Solve the problem? ___yes ___no
    c. Provide an opportunity? ___yes ___no
    d. Meet the needs of stakeholders? ___yes ___no
    e. Be research based? ___yes ___no
    f. List the indicators of progress
       i. Quarterly benchmarks defined
      ii. Report quarterly on progress

The New York School Boards Association (www.NYSBA.org) has a helpful resource that school leaders may want to review. The School Safety Reference Guide was developed in 2018, after the Parkland shooting. Points covered include:

- a Q&A primer on school safety;
- definition of terms used in school safety drills and plans;
- suggested policies and protocol for safety and emergency plans;
- possible amendments to consider in plans so that communication protocols are enhanced;
- definition of personnel titles of safety teams;
- delineation of roles and responsibilities;
- training protocols;
- best practices; and
- collaborative communication protocols.

SUPERINTENDENTS

District leaders have many responsibilities. The primary goal of schools is to educate children. There must be a safe environment conducive to learning, and while ensuring that all personnel prioritize student safety and educational needs, we need to remember that tragedies like the recent school shootings happen infrequently (thankfully) and that a balance of conversation, planning, training, and advocacy is required to keep all stakeholders as safe as possible in schools.

It is the responsibility of the central office staff to ask the right questions, walk campuses to determine priority facility needs, and communicate effectively with school and community leaders, as well as assist the board in advocacy mentioned earlier in this chapter. Finding the resources to support safety initiatives without reducing educational resources for student learning is a great challenge. Superintendents need to be vocal, consistent, and persistent in their advocacy for funding schools effectively.

PRINCIPALS

Principals and their administrative staff members must be able to share their concerns, challenges, and successes with supervisors. There are mandatory safety drills required in every state. Each building must report data from those drill to district offices, who then report information to the state. Advocacy may be needed, especially if any part of the school buildings or campus do not meet required components of safety plans or protocols.

There are many organizations that support building administrators at the state and national level. Advocacy should be individual, district-wide, and through these various organizations as a way of building ongoing support.

TEACHERS

Teachers need to be able to teach their students. Resources for materials and technology that support student learning must be maintained. If resources are reduced, no one benefits, especially the children served. Teachers have many organizations, such as the NEA, where advocacy can be pursued.

STUDENTS

Students need to be encouraged to be vocal advocates. After the Parkland shooting, students formed the #NeverAgain movement and took on the issue of gun control, challenging politicians to take a stand against the National Rifle Association's (NRA) stance on the Second Amendment.

This group of students led a March for Our Lives, in March 2018, that was a global event. It was a march on Washington that had an additional eight hundred sites across the country and world. Students led the charge, for the purpose of tighter gun control and challenges to all to register and vote and get the NRA to back off assault weapon availability and improve background checks for all gun purchases. There were many March for Our Lives events across the country in the summer of 2018 to continue the conversations and student-led protests.

PARENTS

Parents are an integral part of every school district. Schools may have individual Parent Teacher Associations (PTA) or Parent Teacher Organizations (PTO), as well as district-wide organizations. These organizations typically assist schools with fundraising events and celebrations, and work with each building to support students, teachers, and administrators.

Each of these organizations has a national group that local groups are members of, and they can access many services. The National PTA (www.pta.org) has an advocacy resource link and legislative updates posted. The National PTO (www.pto.org) provides links and resources that help parents in their community.

Both of these organizations can assist parent groups in their role and with school personnel. The PTA site has advocacy training manuals and programs and an advocacy toolkit that can assist parents in all aspects of advocacy, as well as guides for dealing with politicians on school issues. There are templates for contacting your politicians on issues, and recommendations for ensuring a response.

The PTO site contains helpful resources on how parents can be engaged in various school and district committees, and how their voices can be heard in a productive manner. Parents can talk online with other parents on things that matter, and get assistance from other parent groups.

Both of these organizations assist parents in staying engaged and involved at various levels in schools and with school issues. These resources are available for free, and have some great ideas for keeping the conversation that matters most as part of a district's ongoing communication efficacy.

COMMUNITY MEMBERS

Engagement of community members occurs through many types of building-level and district events in all school communities. Focusing assistance on school safety matters is a shared concern for many. Think about realtors in a geographical area. If a tragedy occurs, interest of folks moving to that community, house sales in that community, business in stores in that community all wane.

The economic impact of a school shooting cannot be overlooked. It is a way to engage community members in developing effective policies for school safety.

COUNSELORS

School safety is largely dependent on proactive intervention and the ability of schools to have trained counselors (guidance counselors, school social workers, school psychologists) who can provide ongoing and emergency service to children. These staff members are often the ones disengaged students go to and expect assistance from to resolve issues in school, with peers, at home, or in the community. These groups of professionals must advocate strongly for the need of these positions in schools, and must be supported by all other constituent groups mentioned above.

When these services, considered nonmandated, are not funded in schools or in communities, things happen that may have been avoidable. While there are no guarantees, there is research that supports the fact that school counselors available to students are a great help. Violence-prevention programs, positive behavior interventions, and student hotlines to report concerns are just a few of the many suggestions of the National Association of School Psychologists as a way of making our schools safer and helping students deal with various challenges.

Students want to be heard; someone has to be able and willing to listen. These supportive positions help connect students with school and outside sources of support, family support, and a place to seek help.

Mental health services should be clustered on school campuses. These services provide valuable support to students, staff, faculty, families, and community members. If services are located in collaboration between schools and community services, location matters. Easy access to services matters.

COMMUNICATION

The importance of school leaders communicating with all stakeholders cannot be overstated. Too often, lots of conversation occurs right after an event. The challenge is for school leaders to provide ongoing and sustainable conversations so that the school community hears that priorities of school safety are not forgotten by building, district, or community leaders. Forums on school safety are typically held after a tragic event. They should be held on a regular basis, around topics of school climate, school facilities, preparation, drills, and context.

We need to listen to the voices of experience.

Columbine High School, Columbine, Colorado, 1999:

Rachel Scott was the first student killed, seventeen years old. Her brother Craig, sixteen, survived the shooting. Their parents said, "You can lose children two ways. Rachel died, but we could lose Craig, too, if he is not restored emotionally." The parents sold their home, moved, and started a foundation called Rachel's Challenge. Rachel's Challenge is an organization that works to reduce violence, and programs in high schools across the country support this program. (*Denver Post*, 2000)

Virginia Tech, Blacksburg, Virginia, 2007:

Lisa Hemp survived the shooting due to her classmates saving her life. She thought she was "underserving of being recognized as a survivor because she wasn't shot." She was diagnosed with post-traumatic stress disorder (PTSD) and describes how difficult recovering from trauma is and the impact on her life and life work. (Voices of School Shooting Survivors Project, VICE.com)

Sandy Hook Elementary School, Newtown, Connecticut, 2012:

Parents describe their children on CBS (members of Sandy Hook Promise):

"Ana was 6 years old. She taught me about how to love, how to give. She was beautiful and every day I cry." —Jimmy Greene

"Ben was 6 years old. He has a brother Nate. Nate was hiding when he heard Ben and his classmate and educators get shot." —Francine Wheeler

"We lost our sweet little Daniel. He was known as the kid who would talk to somebody sitting alone." —Mark Barden

"Dylan was always smiling. He was six, always smiling and laughing." —Nicole Hockey

"Jesse was six years old. He was my best friend and buddy." —Neil Heslin

"Mary was the school psychologist for 18 years and truly believed that was the place she was meant to be." —Bill Sherlach

"Lauren grew up knowing she wanted to be a teacher and work with children. She had an innocence about her and a kind of denial of all the ugly things in the world." —Terri Rousseau

(Excerpts from CBS News transcript, April 2013)

Marjory Stoneman Douglas High School, Parkland, Florida, 2018:

#NeverAgain movement initiated. March for Our Lives organized. Millions of dollars raised.

Students vocal about political movements standing against the NRA and support through voting for politicians who will make changes in gun-control laws. Parkland survivors took immediate action.

"Us students have learned that if you actively do nothing, people continually end up dead, so it's time to start doing something." —Emma Gonzalez, Parkland survivor

"We can't ignore the issues of gun control that this tragedy raises. And so, I'm asking, no demanding, we take action now." —Cameron Kasky

These are just a few of the many voices we must hear and listen to about the issues and results of school shootings. The children and adults who have been killed, those who have survived with physical and/or emotional wounds, the family members left behind, all must be paid attention to as political action is taken.

Advocacy can take many forms and be done by various members of school communities. The more everyone understands and advocates for school safety issues, the more everyone will be heard in bureaucratic and political venues. The students from Parkland started a movement that needs to be continually discussed.

Voices must be constant, ongoing, and sustainable through the various advocacy opportunities and groups. Change is possible, and there is power in numbers.

Never again.

REFERENCES

California Education Code. Title 1, Division 1, Part 19, chapter 2.5, Article 5.

New York Education Law. Chapter 16, Title II, Article 55, Section 2801.

Rajan, S., Vasudevan, L. V., Ruggles, K. V., Brown, B., & Verdeli, H. (2017). Commentary: Firearms in K–12 schools: What is the responsibility of the education community? Teachers College Record. Retrieved October 31, 2018, from ttps:// masclab.files.wordpress.com/2017/10/rajanetal_firearms-in-k-12-schools.pdf.

Sanchez, R. (2018, February 26). Superintendents in Lower Hudson Valley call for stricter gun laws: View. *lohud.* Retrieved from www.lohud.com/story/opinion/ contributors/2018/02/26/want-safe-schools-cut-acess-guns-increase-access-mental-health-care-view/373592002.

Stewart, J. (2018). Take it from an educator: Arming teachers is not the answer to keeping our students safe. Talking points. Retrieved October 31, 2018, from www.the74million.org/article/take-it-from-an-educator-arming-teachers-is-not-the-answer-to-keeping-our-students-safe.

RESOURCES

www.nyssba.org/clientuploads/nyssba_pdf/school-safety-ref-guide-05012018.pdf
www.nasisp.org/uploads/AdvoacyChecklist_April2016.pdf
www.pto.org/topics.html
www.pta.org/home/advocacy/take-action
https://marchforourlives.com/
https://leginfo.legislature.ca.gov/faces/codes_displayText.xhtml?lawCode=EDC&division=1.&title=1.&part=19.&chapter=2.5.&article=5

About the Editor

Dr. Fern Aefsky has more than thirty years of experience as a teacher and administrator (principal, director, assistant superintendent, and superintendent) in public schools. She has been an adjunct professor at various universities for twenty-four years and is currently director of Graduate Studies in Education at Saint Leo University. Her presentations, publications, and research focus on collaboratively working with interdisciplinary teams to increase student success through effective school leadership and proactive interventions for school stakeholders. Developing programs in higher education that meet the needs of school practitioners through collaborative work is a passion for professional growth and development.

About the Contributors

Dr. Robert Diemer is a retired career law enforcement officer with over forty-three years of varied investigative experience. Dr. Diemer has served as a deputy sheriff, state coordinator for the Florida Sheriff's Association Statewide Task Force, and chief of investigations for the Florida Department of Environmental Protections' Division of Law Enforcement. Dr. Diemer was also responsible for managing and coordinating the operations of the Florida Department of Environmental Protections Environmental Terrorism Response Team. He is nationally recognized for his law enforcement experience, guest lectures throughout the United States, and is an adjunct instructor at several universities.

Dr. Susan Kinsella is dean of the School of Education and Social Services and professor of human services at Saint Leo University. Dr. Kinsella earned her PhD in social work from Fordham University, her MSW from Marywood University, and her BSW from Pennsylvania State University. She is HS-BCP certified (Human Services Board Certified Practitioner). She has over twenty-five years of teaching and administrative experience in higher education, having developed and taught in undergraduate and graduate programs in human services and social work in Pennsylvania, Florida, and Georgia. She is currently vice president for Pi Gamma Mu, an International Honor Society. Her recent e-textbook is titled *Human Services: A Student Centered Approach*. She was elected Social Worker of the Year by the Clinical Social Work Association of Savannah in 2015 and was awarded for her work with Pi Gamma Mu at the last triennial convention.

Dr. Jodi Lamb obtained her doctorate from the University of South Florida. She has over twenty-eight years of experience in medium and large public school districts in elementary, middle, and high schools and district offices. She served as a media specialist, coach, professional developer, assistant principal, and principal. She traveled nationally as a training consultant before becoming an adjunct professor for three different universities. She now holds a full-time faculty position at Saint Leo University. She is currently associate professor and serves as the associate director for graduate education.

Dr. Cindy Lee is a licensed clinical social worker with over thirty-three years of social work practice experience at the direct and administrative levels in the practice areas of individual, couple, and family services. She has expertise in trauma, critical incident debriefing, and compassion fatigue. Dr. Lee is currently the director of the Saint Leo Master of Social Work Program. She has published in the areas of distance education, trauma, compassion fatigue, and values education. Dr. Lee has presented workshops on compassion fatigue, cultural sensitivity, trauma-informed practice, and distance education.

Dr. Karin May has over twenty-five years of law enforcement experience and is currently a reserve captain with a local law enforcement agency. Dr. May also served as a statewide lieutenant assigned to the Florida Attorney General's Office, overseeing elder abuse for Florida's sixty-seven counties. She presented an emergency operations protocol to the attorney general, which was adopted, making Florida the first Medicaid Fraud Agency in the country to respond to affected health care facilities' needs during natural disasters. Karin is nationally recognized in the area of elder abuse and provides national training.

Dr. Debra Mims graduated from Northcentral University with her doctorate in business with a concentration in criminal justice. She is assistant professor of criminal justice at Saint Leo University and a retired Tampa police officer.

Dr. Veronika Ospina-Kammerer graduated from Florida State University's School of Social Work with a DPhil in marriage and the family, and a postgraduate degree in nursing pedagogy. She is professor of social work at Saint Leo University. Her specializations are in gerontology, traumatology, posttraumatic stress, disaster relief work, and international hospice.

Dr. Rhondda Waddell is associate dean and full professor in the College of Education and Social Services at Saint Leo University and is a licensed clinical social worker. Dr. Waddell has more than thirty years of social work practice and membership in the National Association of Social Workers (NASW) organization with a special interest in research, animal-assisted therapy, and interdisciplinary practice.

Dr. Courtney Wiest has a doctorate in post-secondary education leadership and a master's in social work and is a full-time assistant professor in the MSW program at Saint Leo University. Dr. Wiest's current research interests are: higher education and online learning, particularly related to "sense of community" in the online environment; trauma-informed care; and community-based trauma-informed model.

Dr. Nancy Wood is graduate director of the Human Services Administration program in the College of Education and Social Services at Saint Leo University and holds a PhD in human services. Dr. Wood has instructed various courses in human services, social policy, community outreach, management, and social research, as well as developed courses on these topics. Dr. Wood has presented at both national and international conferences on the topic of critical thinking strategies, online pedagogy, human services, ethical leadership, and community relations, as well publishing on these topics.

Dr. Toni Zetzsche earned a bachelor's degree in criminology, a master's degree in elementary education, and a doctorate degree in educational leadership. Dr. Zetzsche has worked eighteen years in public education as a teacher, behavior specialist, assistant principal, and principal. Currently, Dr. Zetzsche is a transformational school-based principal at River Ridge High School in Pasco County, Florida.